# The Bridesmaid's
# GUERRILLA
# Handbook

# The Bridesmaid's GUERRILLA Handbook

SARAH STEIN
AND LUCY TALBOT

BERKLEY BOOKS, NEW YORK

This book is an original publication of The Berkley Publishing Group.

THE BRIDESMAID'S GUERRILLA HANDBOOK

A Berkley Book / published by arrangement with
the authors

PRINTING HISTORY
Berkley trade paperback edition / April 1997

The Putnam Berkley World Wide Web site address is
http://www.berkley.com/berkley

ISBN: 0-425-15676-1

BERKLEY®
Berkley Books are published by The Berkley Publishing Group,
200 Madison Avenue, New York, New York 10016.
BERKLEY and the "B" design
are trademarks belonging to Berkley Publishing Corporation.

PRINTED IN THE UNITED STATES OF AMERICA

10  9  8  7  6  5  4  3  2  1

To Alison, Ilene, Debbie, Risa, and Stephanie—for when it's your turn; and to Steven, who in the middle of this wonderfully vindictive and spiteful project asked me to marry him and changed my whole perspective.

—S.S.

To my mother and father, who taught me to be a lady. And to the dashing Turk Nance, who likes it when I'm not.

—L.T.

# ACKNOWLEDGMENTS

We'd like to thank the following people for their assistance in putting together this project: all of the former bridesmaids who shared their ridiculous, obscene, and sometimes disturbing war stories with us; Sarah's mom, Margery Schab, who donated her wonderful photographic talent and her laser printer; our fabulous agent, Gordon Kato, who played the bad guy for a couple of professional bad guys; and our editor, Jennifer Lata, whose advice and insight into the wackiness of weddings were invaluable.

# CONTENTS

# INTRODUCTION

*A happy bridesmaid makes a happy bride.*

—ALFRED, LORD TENNYSON

*Penelope staggered into her apartment at six P.M. on a Sunday evening, clutching a satin shoe with a broken heel in one hand and a crushed hat in the other. She could see her roommate, Melissa, on the couch in the living room, tuned into 60 Minutes. The sound of the news program's ticking stopwatch resounded in her throbbing head. Penelope moaned all the way into the room and collapsed into her favorite vintage bean bag. Alarmed, Michelle muted the television and jumped from the couch in horror. "What happened?" Penelope, always perfectly pulled together, resembled a Southern belle whose tea party had just been ambushed by the Mad Hatter. "I've been to Emily's wedding," she murmured. "Oh, yes," nodded Melissa, "and you were a bridesmaid." She stood and walked to the Ikea wet bar and poured Penelope a brandy.*

IF YOU'VE opened this book, it's likely that you, like eleven million other women each year, have been handpicked to perform the sacred duties of a bridesmaid by a close friend or relative who is a bride-to-be. It's akin to a universal female draft; from ages eighteen to thirty-five, every woman lives with the awareness that she will be recruited. Inevitably, you will be selected to join the ranks of trusted and forbearing souls who will escort a bride and groom from the rowdy halls of singlehood to the threshold of marital bliss. You are already, or are soon to be, one of the chosen, the proud, and taffeta bedecked. You've heard the war stories and are either eager to be initiated, or resigned to the duty and anxious to get it over with.

Unlike other kinds of recruitable service positions for which you receive highly specialized training before being dropped into the field, a bridesmaid's duties tend to be somewhat ambiguous. Most often, the bride tells you where to pick up your dress (which is akin to a uniform in that it is sure to camouflage all your positive attributes) and when to show up. The bridesmaid waits, fidgets, and then reacts to all that is imposed upon her.

Let's face it: the self-respecting bridesmaid needs to know more.

Why be passive when you can be proactive? This handbook will be indispensable to you throughout the bride's engagement period. Everything you'll ever have to know about surviving as a bridesmaid is now at your fingertips. Keep it on your night table and carry it in your handbag or knapsack, for a bridesmaid's mission is not completed until the newly wedded couple is whisked away from the reception. You are on call 24 hours a day, seven days a week, and you must be prepared for any crisis or turn of events.

Although she is one of the most important players in the wedding pageantry, the bridesmaid often receives less guidance and direction than the busboys at the reception. As integral as her role is to the success of a wedding, there has never been a book exclusively for bridesmaids, one that instructs a woman on how to perform this function successfully. It's not just about knowing when to give the obligatory *oohs* and *aahs* and commiserating with the other attendants about the unflattering décolletage of your matching dresses. It's about support, dependability, and consideration. In fact, the actions or inactions of a bridesmaid throughout the engagement period and up through the wedding reception can affect the mood of the entire event and can quite often cement or sever future relationships with the bride and groom. It is a responsibility not to be taken lightly.

This book clearly defines those responsibilities and will help you perform them with grace, poise, and efficiency. Will it help you to look good in *any* bridesmaid gown, no matter what the cut? Not likely. Will it prevent irksome guests from smiling at you sympathetically and saying, "Always a bridesmaid, never a bride"? Doubtful. What this book *will* do is help make the engagement period and wedding ceremony smooth and pleasurable for the bride, while making them as enjoyable, inexpensive, and hassle-free as possible for you.

# The Bridesmaid's
# GUERRILLA
# Handbook

# CHAPTER ONE
# The Call

BEFORE THE issuance of the regulation martial equipment that identifies individuals of diverse backgrounds commonly as soldiers—the steel helmet, the gas mask, the cartridge belt, the canteen, the first-aid kit, the ammunitions and arms—there is the mobilization. And before the mobilization, there is the draft.

*"I'm engaged!"*

These are two of the most powerful and emotionally charged words you'll ever hear come out of a friend's mouth. For you, these words are fraught with excitement, anticipation ...

*"I want you to be a bridesmaid!"*

... and dread.

We all know what it means to be someone's bridesmaid. Many of us have done it before, others have just heard the stories. Tales of matching dresses in horrific colors with uncomfortable shoes dyed to match. Bad hairdos and expensive bridal showers. Humiliating moments of being paraded down a long aisle like some child's poorly dressed dolls. Other people's relatives staring, pointing, sometimes groping. A florid-faced uncle urging you to jump higher to catch the bouquet so you don't end up a spinster. Oh, what joy! So, you reply with:

*"What an honor! I'd love to be your bridesmaid!"*

# THE ORIGINS OF THE BRIDESMAID

Contrary to most people's beliefs, the bridesmaid's place in the wedding ceremony is much more important than just marching down the aisle and serving as decorative filler in photos. Bridesmaids serve an extremely useful and critical function in the wedding ceremony and the engagement period leading up to it.

As far back as the ancient Greeks, the bridesmaids' place in the wedding ceremony was celebrated for the joy and happiness they contributed to the event. In the days of antiquity, most women were married by the time they turned sixteen; the first bridesmaids were a group of older married women (old biddies of at least 24 or 25) who escorted the young, inexperienced bride to the ceremony as well as throughout the marriage process. Since just about everything served some symbolic purpose to the Greeks, it was believed that if fertile, happily married women escorted the young bride, their good fortune would extend to her. This entourage was also believed to stave off evil spirits until the marriage was completed.

In Anglo-Saxon times, it was considered "unmaidenly" for a bride to enter into marriage willingly and it was common practice for prospective brides to be "captured" by their future husbands. Hence, it was necessary (if only for maintaining appearances) for a bride to gather her friends to protect her from this possibility. These early bridesmaids helped fend off inappropriate suitors or, if the bride preferred, aided the groom's efforts in whatever way possible, while still maintaining the facade of unwillingness. Conversely, the best man was a friend of the groom who helped him capture the object of his affections. As it was possible in those days of reaping and sowing that the young woman might have a brother the size of a linebacker, it was necessary for a marriage-minded man to choose the "best man" for the job. So the earliest "best men" were often quite strapping (not exactly bad news for the bridesmaids).

## THE IMPORTANCE OF THE BRIDESMAID IN THE MODERN CEREMONY

Nowadays, with so many men opting for an *à la carte* lifestyle rather than the commitment of a *prix fixe* meal, fewer brides need assistance fleeing from a determined suitor. Because the function of the bridesmaid has changed so dramatically over the centuries, it is necessary to redefine her duties as they pertain to the realities of today's society. If you're lucky, you'll still have to fend off hulking young men in the name of virtue at the reception, but your new official task is to perform a range of services and functions that will assist the bride through the modern marriage process. You are a member of her crisis management team, her advisory council, and her social committee. She will cry on your shoulder, call upon and disregard your good taste when making decisions about color schemes and flower arrangements, and expect you to dance with her sweaty-palmed second cousin. But you love her and you have to say yes.

As a bride prepares to commit herself to sharing the rest of her life with one man, she calls upon her closest loved ones to assist her. Whereas the bride has a choice when asked the question that will lead her to the altar, the friend or relative asked to participate in the ceremony as a maid of honor or bridesmaid cannot say no. (If you fancy yourself a rebel, go directly to Chapter Twelve, "Just Say No.") It is considered an honor to be offered a supporting role in the big event, yet it is the rare bride who realizes how much she is actually asking of her friend or relative.

The bridesmaid is an emotional ballast, a troubleshooter, and a hostess. The wedding celebration is a momentous occasion; participating in the ceremony and related festivities entails a significant investment, both financially and emotionally. Ideally, the resulting memories will justify the necessary expenditure and the often accompanying stress. While spending money on travel, the bridesmaid dress, matching shoes and accessories, and gifts is usually unavoidable, knowing in advance exactly what is expected of you during your term as a bridesmaid will help to reduce this stress. It's also not a bad idea to find out as soon as possible who the other recruits are—*before* you agree to dress like them, coordinate schedules with them, and march with them.

---

SUPERSTITIONS/TRADITIONS:    Bridesmaids and ushers dress alike (preferably similar to the bride and groom) because it is supposed to confuse any evil spirits who are intent on harming the bride and groom. The tradition also evolved because wedding processions in Europe used to run from the Bride's home, through the village. Dressing alike insured that if the wedding party ran into a jilted ex, he wouldn't know on whom to put "the whammy."

---

# CHAPTER TWO

# The Tour of Duty Begins

BEFORE A tour of duty, an army division undergoes a combat training course. During this grueling period, soldiers are required to run obstacle courses, perform calisthenics, view propaganda films, and stomach "Welcome" speeches by the commanding general. A frequent complaint of soldiers during this time of waiting is that they are seldom told exactly what they'll have to do in combat and are forced to speculate until the need arises for their services. The object is to toughen the recruits both physically and mentally, to prepare them for decision making in hardship and battle, and to weed out the loonies who could prove to be a liability to the others.

You've graciously accepted the invitation to be a bridesmaid, an active and willing participant in the wedding ritual. You're overcome with sentiment, you're *filled* with joy, you're positively BRIMMING with anticipation . . . you're CLUELESS as to what the hell you're actually supposed to do.

Pledging to be a bridesmaid is not the equivalent of signing up for an afternoon of wearing white gloves and sipping mint juleps at a sorority shindig. It is a formidable responsibility and an implicit social contract that must be upheld. There's a lot of grunt work that goes along with the title; in order to maintain a sense of dignity, you'll need to know, long before the rehearsal dinner, what is expected of you.

## WHAT NOW?

Once you've joined the ranks of bridal attendants, it's important you accept that for the duration of the engagement your life will take a back seat to The Wedding. Oh sure, the bride will feel sorry for you when you cry to her about your boyfriend of three years getting transferred across the country, but it had better not interfere with your showing up for your fitting. Like any service for which you enlist, once you accept the mantle of the bridesmaid, you are bound to all duties and functions of the position for the time period set by those in positions of authority—in this case, the bride. It could be three months, it could be two years. For however long the engagement lasts, you are the bride's attendant until the moment you close the door on the limo and wave *bon voyage* to the newlyweds.

Now that you've signed on the proverbial dotted line, you need to prepare yourself for the skirmishes that may lie ahead. Information is your best weapon in the trenches, and it's important that you realize it's not enough just to purchase the designated gear and show up. A loved one has invited you to take an active role in her wedding—W-Day, the most important 24 hours in *her* life. Boy, do you have your work cut out for you.

## RESPONSIBILITIES AND DUTIES OF THE BRIDESMAID

The primary function of a bridesmaid is to help smooth the passage from singlehood to marriage for the bride. This purpose, throughout the ages, has remained unchanged. However, with the elaboration and formalization of weddings over the centuries, the responsibilities have become somewhat more complicated. In every wedding there are the customary duties of the attendants and then there are the bride's interpretations and preferences, which can be anything but customary. A bride should not assume that her bridesmaids know what is expected of them, and her bridesmaids should not hesitate to ask. However, there are the right questions to ask, such as "What color will the bridesmaid dresses be?" and "Will accommodations be provided?" and then there are the questions to which the savvy attendant should already know the answers. If you're asking "Do I pay for my dress?" "Who throws the bridal shower?" and "Can I drink while standing in the receiving line?" and these questions don't seem inappropriate to you, then you need this book.

## Customarily, the Bridesmaid:

- **Offers to run errands and generally assist the bride in any reasonable way with wedding plans.**
- **Helps the maid or matron of honor plan the bridal shower and provides equitable financial contribution.** See Chapter Five, "The Bridal Shower."
- **Records all gifts and their respective givers at the bridal shower.** We all know that in the heat of the moment, gifts get ripped open and cards get separated. Keeping a record of who gave what will ensure that the bride can properly thank all of her guests after she gets the loot home.
- **Helps address wedding invitations.** You may not be asked to do this, since many people use a calligrapher to address their invitations. However, it is part of your job. The outside envelope is hand-addressed in black ink and hand-stamped. Choose flower or bird stamps and refrain from affixing images of dead movie stars or pop musicians to the tasteful, heavy-stock envelope. The sender's return address is written in the upper left-hand corner of the front of the envelope. Keep in mind that in today's high-tech age, there are calligraphy programs available for your computer that are ideal for this purpose. If you get called upon to help with this tedious duty and your handwriting isn't very good, you may want to suggest to the bride that she consider this alternative. If you and the bride don't have access to a computer, contact a local computer center.
- **Attends all pre-wedding parties and related events.**
- **Functions as a co-hostess at the wedding and pre-wedding festivities.** This does not mean that you have to go around to

every guest at the wedding, introducing yourself and offering to freshen drinks. What this does mean is that if anyone is expected to participate actively in the wedding, it's a member of the bridal party. You are on the front line at the wedding and at all pre-wedding events. Think of yourself as part of the "in crowd," one of the "popular" people—at least with regard to the wedding functions. You have a responsibility to be friendly to the other guests and dance. Basically, if the guests see you having fun, they'll want to play too.

- **Pays for her own bridesmaid dress and bridesmaid accessories.**
- **Pays for her own hair styling and makeup.** Sure, you want to look beautiful for your friend or sister's big day. If you don't just wake up that way, you may need professional help. If you live in the town where the wedding is taking place, you probably already have someone you trust to call on. If you live out of town, talk to the bride and get some recommendations. Be clear on one thing, though—unless the bride specifically offers to pay your primping costs, this expense will come out of your own pocket.
- **Arranges for her own transportation to and from the ceremony and the reception.** Unless the bride has made specific arrangements for the attendants ahead of time, you are responsible for getting yourself to and from the ceremony and the reception. It's often helpful to carpool with the other bridesmaids.
- **Pays for her own accommodations.** If you are traveling from afar, it is the bride's responsibility to make arrangements for your accommodations during the wedding. Typically, your options will include staying with a nearby relative or lodging at a local hotel where the bride has reserved a block of rooms for wedding guests. If you opt to stay with the relative, your stay is complimentary, except for the obligatory chit-chat. If a quiet hotel room is more to your liking, expect to pay the bill yourself. Ask if the hotel is offering a discount; many provide special rates for wedding guests.
- **Precedes the bride in the processional.** See Chapter Nine, "At the Wedding."
- **Helps the maid of honor with the bride's bustle.** If the maid of honor is all thumbs, it is likely that this duty will fall on

your shoulders. Find out ahead of time if the maid of honor needs your assistance so that you can attend one of the bride's dress fittings and have a saleswoman at the salon show you how to do it.

- **Greets guests in the receiving line.** If there are more than 50 guests at the wedding, the bridal party will be expected to form a receiving line to meet and greet them. The maid of honor stands after the groom, and the bridesmaids beside her. After the first half hour, bridesmaids may disperse while the bride and groom and their mothers continue to stand in the line. (See Chapter Nine, "At the Wedding.")

- **Sits with ushers at the head table.** If there is a head table, tradition states that the bridesmaids and ushers should sit alternately. If attendants have spouses or live-ins, they can sometimes sit at the head table also. The only real rule is that you should sit boy, girl, boy, girl. Also, if the attendants aren't seated with the bride and groom, make sure that you are seated close enough to the bride so you can reach her conveniently should she need you (such as if her cake falls into her décolletage and she doesn't notice it), and that you are available to participate in the toasts.

- **Dances with her designated usher during the newlyweds' first dance.** So what if the usher who escorted you down the aisle is 5'4" and you're six feet tall? When the music begins and the bandleader calls you to the floor, you are there with a smile on your face and a spring in your step.

- **Participates in the bouquet toss.** This is, of course, the most demeaning of all the wedding rituals. It implies that single women will do just about anything to catch a man—and, well, that's just not a very modern perspective. However, should the bride want to toss her bouquet in traditional fashion to a grouping of maidens, so be it. It's your job to be there, with your hands in the air.

### The Bridesmaid's Wedding Survival Kit

While the items in the preceding list are typical responsibilities of a bridesmaid, every bridesmaid should know that sometimes the call to arms means more than just following standard regulations.

The purpose of being an attendant is to attend to the bride; she is your cause. The finest guerrillas are equipped for any complications or nuisances that can arise at or before the wedding. You are the bride's emergency hotline. Be ready for *any* emergency—medical or otherwise. Prepack a small bag or box with the following items, which may save you or the bride at a critical moment. This will be your Wedding Survival Kit. The contents should include the following:

- **Aspirin and/or ibuprofen.** Boring toasts, lots of drinking, loud music . . . throb, throb, throb . . . get the picture?
- **Band-Aids.** Uncomfortable shoes, dancing, corns. . . . Bring several different sizes and shapes for cuts and blisters.
- **Nasal spray.** Especially useful at outdoor weddings held at the height of hay-fever season. A runny nose is not attractive on any member of the wedding party.
- **Tissues.** If you do get that runny nose, the back of your hand just won't do, especially when you're expected to shake hands in the receiving line. Also, use a tissue to blot your lipstick and it won't rub off on your teeth.
- **White medical tape.** It's shiny, made of cloth, and almost actually looks like some kind of wedding trimming. Be creative; it's good for lots of things from taping bridal boo-boos to holding down headpiece fabric.
- **Needle, thread, and scissors.** Buttons pop off, hems rip, and tags may need to be removed. If you have the time and the dexterity, these are important items.
- **Safety pins.** Because chances are you won't have the time. Bring them in all sizes! Be prepared for flimsy spaghetti straps, ripped lace, and stretched seams. Bridal gowns and bridesmaid dresses get stomped on, smushed, yanked, and caught on flimsy trellises with cascading greenery. Likewise, one good pirouette on the dance floor and the slit of your dress is exposing your hootie to the world. Safety pins are essential to wedding survival.
- **Nail file.** Ragged nails snag tulle and silk. Snags are bad.
- **Clear nail polish.** Nails chip and pantyhose run. This is a fact of life. Clear nail polish is a sure fix for both situations.
- **Smelling salts.** When emotions run high, such as at a wedding, people keel over.

- **Eye drops.** Tears of joy, a late night out with the girls for the bachelorette party, you're stoned . . . whatever your reason, red veiny eyes ruin photos and don't look nice up close. Eye drops also take the red out of a skin blemish.
- **Hair spray.** Buy a small travel-size bottle of hair spray. It's discreet and very effective for putting windblown hair back in its place. Down hair, down! (Or, in some cities, up hair, up!)
- **Breath spray/breath mints.** If you don't know why we're suggesting these, you're the reason we are.
- **Bobby pins (a.k.a. hair pins).** Bring as many as you can, both big and small. No matter how many pins Jacques-Paul stuck into your elaborate 'do, rest assured that the first time your partner dips you, your hair will spring free.
- **Tampons and panty liners.** We don't care if you just finished your period. Mother Nature loves to play jokes, especially if you're planning on wearing anything white or light-colored.
- **Mirror.** All of that smooching and being smooched is enough to make any flower wilt. Perfect for quick touch-ups for the bride (and yourself!).
- **Condoms.** Because you just never know, and in Girl Scouts you learned to be prepared.

Keep your Wedding Survival Kit under the front pew at the ceremony, in the bride's room at the reception hall, or under your table. Wherever you are, the kit should be within arm's reach. The kit is your best friend (besides the bride).

### Go Team!

As a bridesmaid, be mindful of flagging spirits among the corps. Unreturned phone calls are a tip-off; if you're trying to help the maid of honor plan the bridal shower and all you're getting is a lot of answering machines, quiet outrage may have infected the troops. How much time and money have they been asked to contribute already? Morale boosting can take the form of a group bull session in which each woman can vent her frustrations with the prenuptial process: the tedium of fittings at the bridal salon, the drudgery of finding a brassiere that does its job under an off-the-shoulder dress, the numbing practice of sympathetically listening to the bride's latest litany of complaints. Practical jokes at the bridal shower will relieve tension and promote camaraderie, but you may need a mood elevator sooner. A night of watching movies such as *Father of the Bride* (the original with Spencer Tracy or the remake with Steve Martin) and *Muriel's Wedding* can help keep the hysteria of the wedding ritual in perspective. The lesser-known *Catered Affair* (1956) is fun for some campy laughs—an ambitious Bette Davis plans an extravagant wedding for daughter Debbie Reynolds that her husband, Ernest Borgnine, can't afford. Observe how Davis is no different from any bride's mother.

Sometimes a force much darker than weariness is at work and is making everyone uncomfortable. Nan, who was the maid of honor for a childhood friend, recalls a creepy sister of the bride who liked to joke about the groom's infidelities when the bride was not present. Nan had ethical debates with the other bridesmaids, lay awake in bed a couple of nights, and finally took her friend Annette aside to tell her what her sister had been saying. Annette was unfazed. Her younger sister had always been competitive with Annette, and her jealousy at wedding time had come out full force. Annette was only including her sister in the wedding party in deference to her mother's wishes. Thereafter, Nan and the other bridesmaids gave Annette's sister a wide berth and cheerfully carried on with the wedding preparations. If a malaise is descending upon your fellow guerrillas because of one problem bridesmaid, it's often better to group and discuss than to suppress and splinter. It's beneficial to identify shared values and objectives. This kind of episode can even reinforce your outfit's collective commitment to the cause—the bride's happiness and a victorious W-Day.

Performing as a bridesmaid is a daunting, democratizing task not to be taken lightly. If you're the kind of person who has never been very good at taking a backseat to anyone, acceptance of this post may involve a little bit of an attitude check. However, the payoff can be enormously rewarding. You are an honored guest with a crucial role in one of the most important days in a close friend's or sister's life, and as you'll see, the best service you can provide is to be a really good friend.

# ANATOMY OF A BRIDESMAID

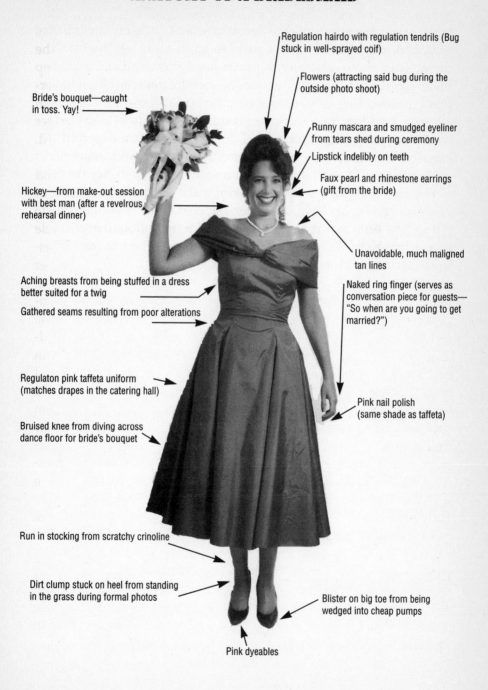

Regulation hairdo with regulation tendrils (Bug stuck in well-sprayed coif)

Flowers (attracting said bug during the outside photo shoot)

Bride's bouquet—caught in toss. Yay!

Runny mascara and smudged eyeliner from tears shed during ceremony

Lipstick indelibly on teeth

Faux pearl and rhinestone earrings (gift from the bride)

Hickey—from make-out session with best man (after a revelrous rehearsal dinner)

Unavoidable, much maligned tan lines

Aching breasts from being stuffed in a dress better suited for a twig

Naked ring finger (serves as conversation piece for guests—"So when are you going to get married?")

Gathered seams resulting from poor alterations

Regulaton pink taffeta uniform (matches drapes in the catering hall)

Pink nail polish (same shade as taffeta)

Bruised knee from diving across dance floor for bride's bouquet

Run in stocking from scratchy crinoline

Dirt clump stuck on heel from standing in the grass during formal photos

Blister on big toe from being wedged into cheap pumps

Pink dyeables

# THE BRIDESMAID'S BUDGET

Weddings are enormously expensive, and playing an integral role in the hoopla will not come cheap. In addition to paying for your dress, your shoes, and any required headpiece, you can expect to incur significant "hidden" expenses, such as transportation to and from the wedding or your share of the bridal-shower budget. The average wedding can cost a bridesmaid upwards of $400 before the bride and groom even say "I do." While certain expenditures can't be avoided, with a little careful planning and some strict budgeting you'll still have enough money left over to pay the rent.

The following is a worksheet with a list of fixed expenses you can expect as a bridesmaid. Enter the cost of each additional expense (the little extras that are, by and large, optional) and create a budget so you know where all your hard-earned money is going.

| DEFINITE EXPENSES | COST | ADDITIONAL EXPENSES | COST |
|---|---|---|---|
| **I. Outfit** | | | |
| A. *Dress* | _____ | E. *Alterations* | _____ |
| B. *Underwear:* | _____ | F. *Accessories:* | _____ |
|   Underpants | _____ |   Necklace | _____ |
|   Bra/Bustier | _____ |   Earrings | _____ |
|   Pantyhose/ | |   Bracelets | _____ |
|     Stockings | _____ |   Gloves | _____ |
|   Garter | _____ | G. *Barrette, headband,* | |
|   Slip | _____ |   *scrunchi®* | _____ |
| C. *Shoes* | _____ | | |
|   Color Dye | _____ | | |
| D. *Headpiece:* | _____ | | |
|   Hat/Horns/etc. . . . | _____ | | |

**II. Bridal Shower** (See Chapter 5)

Fill amount from Chapter 5
worksheet   _____

**III. Bachelorette Party**   _____

**IV. Grooming**

| | | | |
|---|---|---|---|
| A. *Hair* | | B. *Face:* | |
|   Cut | _____ |   Facial | _____ |
|   Styling | _____ |   Professional | |
| | |     Make-up | _____ |
| | |   Waxing (Lip, | |
| | |     Brow, etc.) | _____ |
| | | C. *Body:* | _____ |
| | |   Manicure | |
| | |   Pedicure | _____ |
| | |   Waxing | |
| | |     (Underarms, | |
| | |     Legs, etc.) | _____ |

**V. Travel**

A. *To Wedding:*
  Air fare, Bus fare,
    Train fare,
    Rental Car, Bus,
    Taxicab . . .   _____

B. *Hotel/Motel/Inn*   _____

C. *To Rehearsal*
  *Dinner:*
  Taxi, Rental Car, etc.   _____

D. *To Ceremony:*
  Taxi, Rental Car, etc.   _____

E. *To Reception:*
  Taxi, Rental Car, etc.   _____

F. *Tips for Porters/*
  *Maids/etc.*   _____

*continued*

| DEFINITE EXPENSES | COST | ADDITIONAL EXPENSES | COST |
|---|---|---|---|
| **VI. Gifts** | | | |
| A. Bridal Shower | ———— | C. Engagement | ———— |
| B. Wedding | ———— | D. Baby (for those shot-gun weddings) | ———— |
| **VII. Therapy** | | | |
| A. Therapeutic Swedish Massage | ———— | C. Ten Years of Freudian Psychoanalysis | ———— |
| B. Six visits with an HMO psychologist | ———— | D. Excessive Shoe Shopping | ———— |
| **TOTALS: Definite Expenses:** | ———— | **Additional Expenses:** | ———— |

MONEY-SAVING TIPS

- Most bridal salons will give a discount on the bridesmaid dresses if the bride purchases her wedding gown at their store. Ask the bride to inquire about this when she shops for her gown.
- If the bride asks you to pick out your own dress, consider borrowing one. A friend may have just the right style dress hanging in her closet from a previous wedding.
- Try sample sales; call the showrooms of designers located in your city. Ask to be put on their mailing list so you can be notified when they have a sample sale.
- If you need to take a hotel room, see if any of the other bridesmaids or guests can share the room with you.
- Ask if the bridal shop where the bridesmaid dresses are ordered offers an "early bird special." Some shops will give you a discount on your dress if you purchase it by a certain date.
- White silk and satin shoes get put on clearance racks in January and February.
- Some silk shoes can be re-dyed if you need them to be a shade darker than they already are. Try to recycle the shoes you wore for a previous wedding.
- Do your own hair and makeup for the wedding.

# CHAPTER THREE
# The Maid of Honor

THE FINEST combat leader forges bonds of friendship with the enlisted soldiers but maintains the social barrier that enables her to instruct, to criticize, or to give the orders that may send them into mortal danger.

The greatest honor a bride can bestow upon a woman is the role of maid of honor at her wedding. By conferring this sacred title upon you, she has acknowledged that you are the friend she cannot do without in this world. She likes you a little bit more than any other bridesmaid, she's known you a little longer, she trust you a little more, she believes you to be the most able bridesmaid, she loves you like a sister . . . or you actually are her sister.

## HOW SHE DIFFERS FROM THE OTHER ATTENDANTS

The maid of honor, otherwise known as the honor attendant, is the premier bridesmaid, *La Grande Fromage d'attendants* (translation: The Big Cheese of the attendants). She is second in command only to the bride's mother, and required for even the most modest wedding ceremony, if only to serve as a legal witness. Usually a close girlfriend or relative, she is the bride's confidante and consultant, the assistant wedding coordinator, and the appointed leader of the wedding attendants. In short, the maid of honor is the combat leader who gets to boss around all of the other guerrillas.

There are actually two kinds of honor attendants: the maid of honor and the matron of honor. While essentially the same, the first title refers to a woman who is single and historically "untried," while *matron of honor* refers to someone who is married and (hopefully) has sex on a regular basis. The job description is the same, but tradition dictates this distinction (1) so the best man will know if he can cop a feel during the first dance, and (2) so the women can point and murmur, "What a shame . . . always a bridesmaid, never a bride." Some brides who are sticklers for protocol might ask, "Does this mean my maid of honor has to be a virgin?" Get real. If that were a criterion for being a maid of honor, the term as we know it would cease to exist. Luckily, modern society allows us this slight fudging of terminology so the maid of honor may walk down the aisle confident that she won't be stripped of her title because she is living in sin with one of the ushers.

If you are the maid or matron of honor, the bride will lean most heavily on you throughout her engagement and during the actual wedding reception. You'll be her emotional ballast. You should be prepared to lend a helping hand. The bride's undecided between the lavender taffeta gown with the matching pillbox hat and the ochre tulle with matching bonnet? You're there. To save money, the bride wants to tie ribbons around the napkins at each place setting herself, rather than ask the caterer to do it (there are 400 guests)? You're there. The bride's ex is the Unabomber and she's just received his wedding gift in the mail . . . okay, you shouldn't be *there*, but you get the point.

Sometimes a bride chooses to have both a maid *and* a matron of honor if she is very close to two women—one single, one married—and she doesn't want to favor one over the other. What if both women are single or both are married? The question has been asked if it is inappropriate to have two maids or matrons of honor. While formal etiquette dictates that this is a no-no, we say, "Why not!" Planning a wedding is stressful enough for the bride without her having to choose between two sisters or two friends to fulfill this position of status in her wedding party. No one has ever felt slighted for having to share the title of maid or matron of honor. The importance of the title is not halved simply because the bride cared enough about both women that she wanted each to play a special part in her wedding. If, however, the bride has three or more sisters or friends of equal closeness in her life, please suggest to her that she have you all act as bridesmaids and ask a special relative to stand in as the honor attendant. It's just not chic to have a whole group of women crowding one poor groom. Besides, they'll appear less like honor attendants and more like a posse insuring that the groom doesn't try to skip out.

---

CELEBRITY TRIVIA: Hollywood columnist Louella Parsons served as Rita Hayworth's witness at her civil ceremony in 1949 to Ali Khan at the city hall of Vallauris, France.

---

## RESPONSIBILITIES AND DUTIES OF THE MAID OF HONOR

While it is a bridesmaid's responsibility to take an active role in all pre-wedding and wedding-day festivities, it is the maid of honor who is in charge of actually making and executing many of those plans. The standard duties of the maid of honor are as follows: (Note: the bridesmaid's duties in Chapter 2 not mentioned here also apply to the maid of honor.):

- **Escort the bride on any and all reasonable wedding-related errands.** This does not mean that you must fly to Chicago, if you live in Iowa, to help her find her wedding gown. This does mean, however, that if you live in the same or a neighboring town, you should set aside some mutually convenient time to accompany her on basic errands (gown shopping, bridesmaid gown shopping, choosing invitations, and so on).
- **Initiate the plans for the bridal shower and be the party coordinator.** See Chapter Five, "The Bridal Shower."
- **Help address wedding invitations.** Yes, it sucks, but it's part of your job if requested. Keep in mind that this duty does *not* extend to writing thank-you notes. We know of at least one bride who had the audacity to ask her maid of honor to begin composing her thank-you notes while she was on her honeymoon. The maid of honor is not a secretary. Thank-you notes are a personal expression of gratitude from the recipient

to the giver. The bride and groom should sit down and undertake this chore together. Under no circumstances is it ever appropriate for a bride to delegate this responsibility to a third party. If the bride asks you to do this, pull out this book, point to this paragraph, slam the book shut, and bonk her on the head with it.

- **Choose the gift that the bridesmaids give the bride and collect the money for it.** This additional gift is optional. Many people aren't even aware that an additional gift is sometimes given by the bridesmaids. Use your judgment.
- **Coordinate the fittings of the bridesmaids' gowns.**
- **Hold the bride's bouquet during the ceremony, in addition to her own.**
- **Hold the groom's ring during the ceremony.** Yes, with two bouquets in hand already, it's a lot to carry; try putting it on your pointer finger before the service begins.
- **Serve as a witness, both ceremonial and legal.** The maid of honor is a crucial witness in the wedding ceremony, even if the bride is married by an Elvis impersonator in Las Vegas. Although the maid of honor traditionally signs the marriage certificate, the bride may choose another person to serve as her legal witness on other documents (such as the *Ketubah* in the Jewish religion) in order to allow another friend or family member to play an honored role in the wedding.
- **Straighten the bride's train and veil after the processional and before the recessional.** Many past maids of honor have been overzealous in this task and, when lifting the back of the train to puff it out and straighten it, have exposed the bride's tushy to the guests. This is a wedding, not a livestock auction, and the goods should not be exposed for public viewing.
- **Lift the veil for the husband's kiss, if she is also the bride's sister.**
- **Stand in the receiving line.** If the wedding is larger than 50 people, there will be a receiving line. (See Chapter Nine, "At the Wedding.") Shake hands, smile, be friendly. Exchange pleasantries.
- **Propose a toast during the reception.** Optional. If you start to sweat and break out in hives at the thought of speaking in public, you may want to pass. However, giving a toast is a

wonderful opportunity to express your good wishes to the bride and groom. It's a smart idea to remain relatively sober until after your speech; while a good belt may calm the nerves, no one wants to listen to you go on for 20 minutes about how much you love everyone. (See page 94.)

- **Assist the bride's mother in helping the bride change from her wedding gown into her going-away clothes.** This will also include helping the mother of the bride put the bride's dress away—no small task.

While the preceding responsibilities represent the most traditional duties, there are other functions the maid of honor can perform that are equally indispensable to the bride. As the maid of honor, you can wear many other hats besides a bonnet, including those of:

- **Bustler.** You've seen pictures of those wedding gowns that have trains so long you could park the limo on them, right? How do you think a bride dances at the reception with a parking lot attached to her posterior? She bustles the train. There are several kinds of bustles and it's your job to be able to help her bustle it so that the hem lies evenly all the way around. Make sure you take at least one trip to the bridal salon with the bride so that the saleswoman or tailor can show you how it's done.
- **Platoon leader.** The squad is under your command and they'll look to you for information about the *who*s, *when*s, and *where*s of the wedding. Send a pre-wedding newsletter to each of the bridesmaids. (See the worksheet on page 24.) Use this newsletter to inform the troops where they'll be falling in for the rehearsal dinner, hair and makeup, and pre-wedding pictures. Remind them about scuffing up the bottoms of their new shoes for added traction, make sure each one knows to pick up extra pantyhose, and confirm how each will be transported from the ceremony to the reception. This newsletter is the perfect opportunity to keep everyone in the wedding party apprised of the schedule for the wedding and to ensure that there are fewer slip-ups.
- **Chief information officer.** It's 6:30 P.M. and the guests have begun to arrive—do you know where the officiant is? Make

sure you do. As the assistant wedding coordinator, it is crucial that you carry a copy of the bride's contact list. Fill in the Contact Sheet on page 26 with the contact names and numbers for *all* wedding attendants and service providers including the hairdresser, makeup artist, and so on. Also, carry spare change or a calling card for last-minute phone calls. Don't expect anyone to have loose change on her (taffeta dresses rarely come with pockets). The modern alternative to a germ-covered pay phone? Your own cellular phone.

- **Voodoo practitioner.** If the bride is superstitious, she may put you in charge of making sure the groom doesn't see her in her wedding gown before the ceremony begins; it's bad luck. You should know such mysterious things. For instance, if the groom steps on the bride's gown or veil at the altar, he will dominate the household. If the bride steps on his coat, she'll control their home. The maid of honor or the mother of the bride may drape the bride's veil over the groom's feet, while the best man will take it off and throw it back, ensuring that the man will rule. This power struggle can go on interminably.

- **Checklist holder.** The bride should have a checklist of all the things she'll need on her wedding day: dress, shoes, something old, something new, something borrowed, something blue. A day before the wedding, run through her checklist with her to make sure she has everything she'll need (and will still have a day to pick up anything she doesn't); then run through it again on the day of the wedding before she leaves her house.

- **Bad guy.** While the bride is the commander-in-chief, you're her general on the front line and can make decisions about how to handle minor skirmishes in her stead. Suppose the videographer is handing out his business cards to everyone at the reception, and the band is taking their break just as the happy couple is about to cut their wedding cake. Reprimand the videographer; goose the band. Service people must behave properly and adhere to schedules; they are professionals hired to do a job. You have the authority to keep them in line. The bride shouldn't be pulled out of her first dance or a romantic reverie to play the heavy. As the maid of honor, it's your job to handle on-site crises.

As you can see, your primary goal as the maid of honor is to relieve the bride of having to worry over too many details on her wedding day. This responsibility extends to solving problems that arise, both minor and major. Be prepared for the mundane, such as helping the bride maneuver her hoop skirt into the bathroom stall, as well as for the potentially deadly, such as intercepting the groom's rabbit-boiling ex when she waltzes into the reception uninvited. Many things can go wrong at a wedding and often do. You must be on the alert so the bride can enjoy her day. This is no job for the faint of heart. The key to being a successful maid of honor is a lot of preparation and a very good sense of humor.

TRADITIONS:   In the Christian faith, it is traditional for the maid of honor and best man to be appointed the godparents of the bride and groom's first child.

PRE-WEDDING NEWSLETTER

For the wedding of: _____

Wedding date: _____

# ATTENTION BRIDESMAIDS!

This pre-wedding newsletter contains specific information for the bridesmaids about the details of the rehearsal, the rehearsal dinner, and the wedding. If you have any questions, please call

_____

(your name)

at telephone # _____

## The Rehearsal and the Rehearsal Dinner

The rehearsal will be held at _____ o'clock at:

_____

(location/address)

The rehearsal dinner will be held at _____ o'clock at:

_____

(location/address)

## The Wedding Day

### Primping Schedule:

The following is a list of the bridesmaids who have arranged for hair and makeup sessions and their assigned primping times. We will be primping at:

_____

(location/address)

| **Makeup Schedule** | **Hair Styling Schedule** |
|---|---|
| (time/name) | (time/name) |
| ___:00/_____ | ___:00/_____ |
| ___:30/_____ | ___:30/_____ |
| ___:00/_____ | ___:00/_____ |
| ___:30/_____ | ___:30/_____ |
| ___:00/_____ | ___:00/_____ |

_____:30/_____ _____:30/_____

_____:00/_____ _____:00/_____

At _____ o'clock, we will be dressing for the wedding at:

_____

(location/address)

**Wedding Schedule:**

**Start time** _____

**Meeting place/address** _____

_____

**Photographs** _____

_____

**Ceremony** _____

_____

**Reception** _____

_____

**Transportation:**

Bridesmaid's name          Means of transportation to ceremony

_____

_____

_____

_____

_____

Additional information:

_____

_____

_____

_____

_____

_____

# CONTACT SHEET

|  | Name | Phone Number |
|---|---|---|
| Bride | | |
| Groom | | |
| Mother of the bride | | |
| Father of the bride | | |
| Mother of the groom | | |
| Father of the groom | | |
| Bridesmaid | | |
| Bridesmaid | | |
| Bridesmaid | | |
| Bridesmaid | | |
| Bridesmaid | | |
| Bridesmaid | | |
| Best man | | |
| Usher | | |
| Usher | | |
| Usher | | |
| Usher | | |
| Usher | | |
| Usher | | |
| Officiant | | |
| Readers | | |
| Ring bearer | | |
| Ceremony music contact | | |
| Flower girl | | |
| Caterer / venue | | |
| Band contact | | |
| Florist | | |
| Videographer | | |
| Photographer | | |
| Makeup person | | |
| Hairdresser | | |

# CHAPTER FOUR

# The Bridesmaid's Timetable

IN WAR, there is a direct correlation between having a plan and celebrating victory.

Just as the bride needs to prepare step-by-step for W-Day, so must the bridesmaid and maid of honor. Whether the wedding is a clambake on the beach or a black-tie, sit-down dinner for 350, there is no other celebrated milestone in life that involves so much planning and so many egos. It is an extremely complex and emotionally charged event, with societal laws and cultural mores to observe and expectations to fulfill. Can you understand why the bride is tearing her hair out? Beware the trickle-down effect: freneticism and hypersensitivity can be contagious and may lead to a distortion of reality. After you receive a dozen late-night phone calls from the bride wailing that the florist is not offering her the shades of French tulips he found for her more charismatic older sister, you may find yourself reaching for the phone to gripe to your boyfriend that the bride intentionally chose a tea-length aubergine dress for her bridesmaids so nobody could possibly upstage her. Stop! Don't make the mistake of troubling yourself with imagined motives and don't air to your boyfriend or co-workers the irksome, petty details of the wedding process. Your boyfriend will become allergic to the word *wedding* and your colleagues will avoid you like the plague. The antidote to panic and petty behavior? A rational approach to the larger picture—the timetable.

The surest way to keep the bride sane is to offer her assurance that she can rely on your support. You can't accomplish this by picking up your dress at the tailor's an hour before the photo session. The key to being a successful bridesmaid is planning, planning, planning. Don't assume your shoe-repair shop will correctly dye your white silk pumps the identical rose-petal pink of your bridesmaid dress on the first try, or that your hay fever will take a vacation the day of the wedding. With a little advance preparation, you can glide right through the bride's engagement period with minimal stress, hopefully avoiding those pitfalls that can turn an otherwise joyous event into an excruciating memory. Just because it's not your wedding doesn't mean you don't have to pull your weight. As a bridal attendant, you have accepted a major role in the most important event in someone else's life, and there are about a hundred things you will need to do in order to prepare for the Big Day. The following timetable will help you:

ONE YEAR TO NINE MONTHS BEFORE THE WEDDING DAY:
- Purchase engagement gift (optional).
- Attend engagement party.

SIX MONTHS AHEAD
- Provide your dress measurements to the bride, maid of honor, or designated bridal salon for dress ordering. If you're an OOTA—Out-of-Town Attendant—this time frame will allow for delivery of the dress to your home, leaving plenty of time for alterations and to correct any major mix-ups (such as, you get shipped Cousin Martha's gown and she gets yours—she's a size 16, you're a 6).
- If you're fortunate and the bride asks you to choose your own dress for the wedding, start searching for your gown. Begin this search as early as possible. Believe it or not, stores don't carry summer gowns in the summertime. They carry them in the late winter and spring. Don't wait till the last minute to pick out a dress; the selection will be paltry.
- Start planning the bridal shower (see Chapter Five, "The Bridal Shower").

## THREE MONTHS AHEAD

- Pick up and pay for your bridesmaid gown.
- Take the gown to the tailor for any alterations.
- Purchase your shoes. This allows for plenty of time to have them dyed if they must match your dress.
- Schedule a hairdresser appointment for the wedding day if you're going to have your hair professionally styled (optional).
- Schedule a manicure appointment (if you don't plan to do your own nails).
- Make arrangements for accommodations if you're an OOTA. Hotels fill up quickly, and chances are that even if the bride and groom have reserved a block of rooms at a group rate, there is a deadline for reservations.
- Make plans for the bachelorette party for no less than one week prior to the wedding. (See Chapter Seven, "The Bachelorette Party.") You'll feel queasy enough when nosy guests engage you in conversation about the latest developments in your life without having to tend to the side effects of a hangover as well.
- Maid of honor: Pick out a gift for the bride from the bridesmaids to present to the bride either at the bridesmaid luncheon or the rehearsal dinner. (Optional—see Chapter Three "The Maid of Honor.")

## ONE MONTH AHEAD

- Pick up the altered dress. Try it on *before* you leave the shop!
- Make sure you have appropriate undergarments.
- Plan your outfit for the rehearsal dinner.
- Pick up your shoes at the shoe shop where you had them dyed.
- Pick up any required headgear. If none is required, you may still want to pick up something for your hair, either for the ceremony or for later in the reception. Very few hairdos last a whole evening. You may want to buy a hair band or a barrette that goes with your dress so that you can pull your hair back at the reception.
- Purchase a wedding gift. Technically, you have up to one

year after the wedding to give a gift. Decide if you want to bring a gift to the wedding or if you prefer to send one at a later date. If you've already laid out a great deal of money for this event, you may want to save a little each month and give the couple a gift sometime after the wedding.

- Get your hair cut. Don't get your hair cut on the day of the wedding, or even the day before. A bad haircut can really dampen your spirits. Get your hair cut no less than a month before the wedding and DON'T try anything drastic!

TWO WEEKS AHEAD

- Scuff up your shoes. Take them outside (on a nice day, please) and walk around on the sidewalk or an asphalt road. Do a little soft-shoe number for your neighbors if you like, but scuff up the soles so that when you wear them at the reception, you won't slide on the dance floor and into the punch bowl.
- Attend the bridal luncheon (if the bride is throwing one).
- If you're going to have a facial, do it NOW! We know plenty of overzealous bridesmaids who, in pursuit of perfection for W-Day, have gotten facials a day or two before the wedding day. Bad idea. Yes, your skin will glow, but you'll also have nasty blotches and red marks where the facialist picked, and picked, and picked. Allow time for your face to heal fully.

ONE WEEK AHEAD

- Assemble the contents of your Wedding Survival Kit. (See Chapter Two, "The Tour of Duty Begins.")
- Confirm directions to the ceremony and the reception site.
- Confirm transportation plans to the ceremony and the reception site.
- Confirm transportation home from the reception.
- Make sure you have all additional items you will need for the wedding (pantyhose, hair accessories, gloves and so on). (See "Wedding-Day Checklist," page 86.)

THE DAY BEFORE

- Get a manicure, or do it yourself.

- Press your dress if it needs it, and hang it up where it won't get wrinkled.
- Go to bed early!

THE DAY OF THE EVENT (W-DAY)
- See Chapter Nine, "At the Wedding."

# CHAPTER FIVE
# The Bridal Shower

ADVANCEMENT WITHIN the military institution often points to great success in domestic politics. Ruthlessness and cunning are qualities required for both. Hence, in a reciprocally beneficial relationship, one often glorifies and aggrandizes the other.

The bridal shower is the most well known, and the most feared, of the bridesmaid's responsibilities. The tradition is believed to date back several centuries to Holland, where a young woman was deprived of her customary dowry because her father disapproved of her marriage to a poor miller. Supportive friends and villagers "showered" her with gifts for her new household. Perhaps the Dutch bride received plates, cookware, and a farm animal or two; the gifts certainly reflected the community's intent to give the new bride what she most needed to set up her own home. Such is still the tradition today.

Unlike the straightforward bridal showers of yesteryear, today we attempt to dress up the objective by playing silly games and telling embarrassing stories about the bride's past. We provide the guests with a little entertainment before we thank them graciously for their gifts and send them on their way. The prime directive of showers past and present has remained the same: people get together to give the bride lots of useful loot so she can feather her nest. Rather than villagers banding together, it is now obligatory for the bridesmaids to sponsor this event and solicit gifts on the bride's behalf.

Throwing a bridal shower is a time-consuming and costly venture. For some brides, this is the most important pre-wedding event. Not only do you need to satisfy your own sense of duty by throwing a beautiful party you can be proud of, but you have to take into consideration the bride's expectations of what a shower should be. If she's a sweet, old-fashioned girl who is fond of co-ordinating her headband to her purse, you should think twice before throwing the shower at your favorite local barbecue joint. Remember, this shower is for her; you may have to compromise your personal style a bit to plan an event you'll both remember fondly. Does this mean that when you plan Buffy's shower you must outshine her coming-out party at the Waldorf-Astoria, sac-rificing yourself to the great Visa god? Absolutely not! You can throw all kinds of perfectly wonderful (and tasteful) bridal show-ers to complement a variety of tastes and still have enough money left over to pay your phone bill.

---

SUPERSTITIONS: It's good luck if the first gift the bride-to-be opens is the first gift she uses.

---

## PLANNING THE EVENT

Traditionally, the maid of honor and/or the bridesmaids throw the shower a month or more before the wedding, but very often a relative or the mother of the bride or groom will want to be involved in the planning as well. Although etiquette frowns on an immediate family member hosting the shower, the sad truth is that it can be difficult to recruit assistance for this task. Accept the volunteers who come forward, regardless of blood ties. If you're a woman with a career and a personal life, you'll welcome the extra hands. Have you heard the old tale about the hen who asks everyone in town to help her bake bread and doesn't find a willing participant until the bread emerges fresh from the oven? Planning a party is similar: everyone wants to savor the fruits of your labor, but no one wants to contribute time, energy, or dough. Manners mavens may be sticklers for the rule that bans mothers and sisters from sending the invitations, but we believe that nowadays, with so many brides marrying later in life and paying for their weddings independently, the immediate family's involvement is acceptable. If Mrs. Lowenstein insists on footing the bill when you plan the shower, and you're struggling to make your next car payment, take her up on her offer. Your friend won't love you any less and you won't go broke. Just be sure that Mrs. L. is going to let you plan the shower; accepting money can be a tricky business. Oftentimes, inflexible opinions accompany financial support. If Mrs. L's money has strings attached that are going to cause you migraines, make do with the money you collect from the other bridesmaids along with what you can contribute yourself.

The following advice has been designed to guide you through the bridal-shower planning process and will help you plan an event you and your fellow attendants can be proud of.

---

SUPERSTITIONS: The giver of the first or seventh gift opened will be the next one married.

---

*Six months before the shower, start planning.* Get together with the other bridesmaids and the maid of honor to discuss the basics of the shower. The maid of honor should head up this effort, but don't wait for her to call. If you don't hear from her by at least four months before the wedding, contact her. If everyone lives in the same town, get together for lunch, dinner, or margaritas to discuss ideas for the shower. When all the attendants are old friends, organizing the shower can be a breeze; but five women who have no relationship to one another other than a shared mutual friendship with the bride may not readily cooperate with one another. In fact, the fur can fly. Remember that this shower is for someone you are *all* close to and it doesn't matter if you still blame Jodi for stealing the bride's previous boyfriend. She's forgiven Jodi and moved on (clearly!) and so should you. Now is not the appropriate time for grudges. Resist the temptation of cattiness and focus on the primary objective: an outstanding shower for your friend. Besides, there's plenty of time to verbally bash the offending party after the reception.

*Define your budget.* Whether you're one person or twelve, the budget is the single biggest determinant for the style of shower you will throw. A dinner party is more lavish and expensive. A brunch or tea is also quite elegant, but will be a fraction of the cost. Knowing how much money everyone has to spend will help you make this decision. While it is the maid of honor's duty to head up the efforts behind the shower, you are expected, unless otherwise stated, to contribute both financially and otherwise to the event. When "the sky's the limit," terrific. But in most cases, pooling resources is the best way to put together a great party as inexpensively as possible. Creativity and friendship, more than money, produce the best shower.

If you are throwing the shower alone, consider any resources that may be available to you (your parents' home, a bride's relative's home, your own apartment, and so on) and set a *firm* budget. One maid of honor we know found herself hosting an enormous shower just because the bride's mother had handed her an extensive guest list. Not only did she find herself stuck with the bill, but she was unable to pay her bills that month and her phone was shut off. She was so outraged that she refused to speak to the bride after the wedding; they are no longer friends.

The only person this attendant really had to blame was herself. Don't think that because you're a bridesmaid, you have to throw some elaborate affair because the mother of the bride wants you to (unless of course she's paying for it)—and don't be strong-armed into it. While you should plan an event which will reflect your fabulous taste and your feelings for the bride, a *gracious* bride will be pleased with any effort you make, no matter how inexpensive. If she's not, she's not much of a friend.

What can you do when confronted by an overbearing mother of the bride? Take a stand. We don't suggest throwing a temper tantrum, but you should explain, in no uncertain terms, that you have a fixed budget of X dollars and that you and the other attendants have already decided upon the kind of shower you will be throwing, as well as the guest limit. *Don't Apologize*. Outline your limits and make it clear that while it would certainly be lovely to throw a shower at the most expensive restaurant in town, unfortunately it's not within your budget. Don't be afraid to remind her tactfully that a bridal shower is a present for your friend and although it is traditional, technically it is not obligatory (believe it or not). The shower is your gift to the bride. The bride's mother wouldn't insist on helping you pick out your wedding gift for the couple, would she? A shower is a ritual expression of your concern that the bride have what she needs for her new home, and it is inexcusable for the mother of the bride to impose her standards on how you express that concern. Set your limits in the beginning, be realistic, and stick to them.

TRADITIONS: Save the ribbons from the shower gifts and use them to make a mock bouquet for the bride-to-be to carry during the rehearsal. (See Chapter Eight, "The Rehearsal and Rehearsal Dinner.") After the rehearsal, the bride tosses this faux bouquet and whoever catches it will be the next to marry. (The origin of this is unclear, but it is believed that these ribbons represent the bride's fertility. We have no idea why, but who wants to argue with tradition?) Some bridesmaids collect the ribbons and use them to stuff a "good luck" pillow for the bride.

*Divide up the responsibilities and expenses.* The key word for a successful shower is *equity*. Don't assume that the matron of honor is going to foot the bill just because she's a Kennedy twice removed. It's not fair for one person to be expected to contribute $500 while someone else only puts in $50, just because she has more money—unless, of course, she offers. If someone is severely strapped for cash, she can contribute additional services, such as addressing invitations or baking the shower cake. Everyone needs to be very clear *up front* about what she can contribute so that no one feels that she was taken advantage of later on. If one of the bridesmaids is a phenomenal baker and another has a large space in which to throw the party, take that into account. Add up the contributions, including your budget, and you'll have your guide-

TRADITIONS:   In some regions of the country, it is customary for one of the bridesmaids to volunteer to make a hat for the bride-to-be out of the discarded gift wrappings. Cardboard from a box top usually makes up the base of the hat; a small sample from each gift is used (either the ribbon or a scrap of wrapping paper). This practice takes a little more dexterity than making a faux ribbon bouquet, but the hat then serves as a sort of "good luck" memento for the bride. Usually the bridesmaids make her wear the "garbage" (as Murphy Brown would say) on her head and then take pictures of her. We have no idea where this tradition began, but we think this may serve as some kind of insurance for the attendants, since the bride almost never gets the negatives.

| Responsibilities | Projected Cost | Actual Cost |
|---|---|---|
| Nonalcoholic beverages | | |
| Liquor | | |
| Food | | |
|   *Salads* | | |
|   *Sandwiches* | | |
|   *Entrées* | | |
|   *Bread* | | |
|   *Munchies* | | |
|   *Crackers and cheese* | | |
|   *Vegetables and dip* | | |
|   *Dessert* | | |
| Location | | |
| Decorations | | |
|   *Balloons* | | |
|   *Theme decorations* | | |
|   *Candles* | | |
| Linens | | |
|   *Tablecloths* | | |
|   *Napkins* | | |
|   *Cocktail napkins* | | |
| Flowers | | |
| Flatware | | |
| Servingware | | |
| Glassware/cups | | |
| Invitations/postage | | |
| Camera/film | | |
| Party games/theme accessories | | |
| Coffee/coffee urn | | |
| Place cards | | |
| Favors | | |
| Cleanup goods | | |
|   *Plastic wrap* | | |
|   *Paper towels* | | |
|   *Plastic bags* | | |
| Shower cake | | |
| Setup | | |
| Cleanup | | |
| Rentals (tables, chairs, and so on) | | |
| Entertainment | | |

IMPORTANT NOTE: SAVE RECEIPTS! After the shower you can tally up your expenses and ask individuals for any unexpected, additional expenses. Discuss doing this at the onset of planning so that everyone expects it later on and is prepared. Nothing is more awkward than discussing finances with virtual strangers; the fewer surprises, the better.

lines for the shower. Use the list of responsibilities on page 39 to keep track of responsibilities and expenses, and divvy them up accordingly.

*Pick a date and time.* The key to planning any party, big or small, is to set the time and date. The date is crucial because it gives you a goal to work for and is your first established element of the party. The time will define the style of the shower: 7:30 P.M. for cocktail party or dinner; 3:00 P.M. for a tea party; 12:00 noon for a brunch. Keep in mind that most showers are thrown anywhere from two months to three weeks before the wedding. Whether the party is a surprise or not, make sure you clear the time and date with the bride's mother and fiancé. You don't want to go through the trouble of planning the shower only to find out that the bride will be out of town on business that weekend.

*Compose the guest list.* A bridal shower is a more intimate affair than a wedding; customarily, only close friends and relatives of the bride and groom should be invited. Ask the bride for a list of names and addresses, or, if it is a surprise, get lists from her mother and fiancé. Keep in mind that the bride may be thrown more than one shower and try to avoid inviting people who have been invited to another shower for the same bride. If anyone—for instance, a co-worker—has already been invited to another shower, be thoughtful and make it clear to her that only her presence, not another present, is requested.

*Book the venue and entertainment.* Once you've decided on the time, date, and place, you need to book the space you'll need for the shower. If you are having the shower in a friend's home, obviously, this doesn't apply to you. However, if you are holding the shower in a restaurant or rented space of any kind, you need to reserve the space as early as possible. The same goes for any entertainment you have planned, be it a piano player or a palm reader. You don't want to send out 40 invitations and then find out that the restaurant where you were planning to hold the shower isn't available.

> SUPERSTITIONS: Folklore says that the number of ribbons the bride-to-be cuts while opening her gifts corresponds to the number of children she'll have.

## THE TIMETABLE

Once you have the aforementioned basics set, you're ready to begin planning the details of the shower. The following timetable will give you a general format for you to follow from three months before the shower to the moment the doorbell rings, so that you can plan your schedule, use your time efficiently, and suffer from as little stress as possible during the bridal-shower planning process.

FOUR MONTHS BEFORE
- Call other bridesmaids if the planning has not yet begun.

THREE MONTHS BEFORE
- Purchase the invitations.
- Complete the invitations.
- Reserve rental equipment (tables, chairs, and so on).

SIX WEEKS BEFORE
- Address and mail the invitations.

ONE MONTH BEFORE
- Order any catered food you are planning to serve at the shower.

THREE WEEKS BEFORE
- Regroup with your co-hostesses and confirm responsibilities.
- Discuss whether there will be a gift from the bridesmaids for the bride.
- Choose an outfit!

- Follow up with any invited guests who have not responded.
- Order flowers.

## TWO WEEKS BEFORE
- Confirm delivery of rental equipment.
- Purchase decorations.
- Purchase necessary theme decorations.
- Purchase your personal gift for bride and a card.
- Purchase the bridesmaids' gift for bride (optional).
- Pick up your outfit at the cleaners.
- Book a manicure appointment for the day before the shower.
- Confirm that you have all the equipment you need for the party (see the checklist on page 39).

## ONE WEEK BEFORE
- Check in with your co-hostesses.
- Purchase alcohol and other beverages.
- Cook anything that can be frozen.
- Stock up on ice.
- Make sure you have scissors, tape, pencils, and note pads.
- Be sure you have any necessary items for the games.
- Confirm order and delivery of any catered food.

## TWO DAYS BEFORE
- Begin to decorate.
- Shop for main food items.
- Clean the house (if the shower will be in your home).
- Have the alcohol delivered.

## THE DAY BEFORE
- Shop for fruits and vegetables.
- Clean fruits and vegetables in the morning.
- Iron any linens that may need it.
- Plan the music (optional).

## THE DAY OF THE EVENT

- Have any catered food delivered at least one hour before the party.
- Chop vegetables and fruit.
- Lay out platters and main dishes.
- If the shower is at your home, remove the prescription or recreational drugs from your medicine cabinet.

CELEBRITY TRIVIA: Grace Kelly's seven wedding attendants gave her a bridal shower in March 1956, arranging their gifts under a yellow umbrella that matched the gowns they would be wearing at the nuptials a month later in Monaco. Mrs. Alfred Hitchcock attended.

MONEY-SAVING TIPS

- Have the shower at a home—anyone's home. It's cheaper than a restaurant.
- Make the food yourself. Catered food can get expensive. But if you can barely boil an egg, be fair to your guests and volunteer to be responsible for decorations instead. Then delegate the cooking to the other bridesmaids.
- Instead of fancy centerpieces, use inexpensive potted plants in terra-cotta pots. We recommend ivy; it's cheap and chic.
- Instead of giving fancy chocolate favors with personalized boxes, bake some cookies and brownies ahead of time and freeze them. Package them up in your own little cartons (plenty of gourmet stores sell them and they're not expensive) or pretty tissue paper. Many stores stock do-it-yourself decorating items that make even drab goods look pretty nifty.
- Other cheap favors include tiny potted plants or assortments of exotic tea bags wrapped in ribbon.
- Serve fresh berries instead of elaborate desserts.

# SHOWER THEMES

Although we prefer the old-fashioned "girls only" showers (hanging out with girlfriends is cathartic, and it lends to our *mystique*), many people nowadays insist on inviting both men and women to bridal showers. If this is *really* what you want, then fine, but keep in mind that most men just don't really appreciate the ritual. If you do opt for a co-ed shower, try to gear the shower theme and games toward something both the women and men will appreciate. A Victorian tea makes for a beautiful shower, but very few guys can comfortably hold a teacup.

Whether you decide to have a co-ed shower or a shower for "girls only," having a theme can make a party more personal and add charm as well as provide you with a general guideline for decorations and games. There is no limit to the kinds of shower you can throw; most important, a theme that is chosen to reflect the couple's interests and tastes will guarantee gifts they can use. The following is a list of common, and not-so-common themes.

*Wishing Well.* This is the most traditional of themes and is also often used as an accompaniment to another theme. We like to think of this as a "gadget" shower because it calls for guests to bring a small secondary gift—a gadget—that the couple can use in their kitchen or home. The gadgets (which can be marked with the guests' names, or not) are placed in a small fake well covered in cheap-looking lace or crepe paper (why this design has caught on is beyond us). After the bride opens her other gifts, she opens the treats in the well. That's it. That's the whole theme. The point is to buy little things she won't think to buy but are useful, such as a flashlight, corn holders, a garlic peeler, a mushroom scrubber, an egg timer, a meat thermometer, a melon baller, or a vegetable peeler.

*Time-of-Day Shower.* For this shower theme, each guest is assigned a different time of day (7:00 A.M., 8:00 A.M., 9:00 A.M., and so on) and is supposed to bring a gift that is useful at that hour or reflects the mood of that time of day. It's okay, if you have a lot of guests, to break times into half-hour intervals. This is a great way to ensure that the bride will receive gifts she can use throughout the day. Interesting sample gifts:

7:00 A.M.—massaging shower head
8:00 A.M.—egg cups, breakfast-in-bed tray
9:00 A.M.—cereal bowls, coffeemaker
10:00 A.M.—toaster oven
11:00 A.M.—newspaper subscription
12:00 noon—breadbox
1:00 P.M.—picnic basket
2:00 P.M.—videotape of *Love in the Afternoon* starring Audrey Hepburn and Gary Cooper
3:00 P.M.—afghan throw (nap time)
4:00 P.M.—tea kettle
5:00 P.M.—a foot massager (long day, aching feet)
6:00 P.M.—one or more settings of the registered dinnerware
7:00 P.M.—pizza stone with all of the fixin's (pizza cutter, recipes)
8:00 P.M.—wine glasses
9:00 P.M.—brandy glasses
10:00 P.M.—universal remote for the television
11:00 P.M.—lingerie, sex toys (don't forget batteries)
12:00 midnight—popcorn popper (for late-night munchies)

*Kitchen Shower.* If the bride or groom loves to cook, this is a great idea. Guests bring gifts for the kitchen: pots, pans, griddles, ice-cream makers, waffle irons, place settings, cookbooks, baskets of utensils, and so on.

*Around-the-House Shower.* Each guest is assigned a different room in the house and brings a gift for that room. This will vary the type of gifts the bride receives.

*Lingerie Shower.* (Is the mother of the bride going to be there?)

*Linen Shower.* Guests bring bed linens, towels, and so on, as gifts. Before you throw this kind of shower as a theme, check the bride's registry to see if she has requested this stuff. If she hasn't, stay away from this theme; chances are she'll want to pick her own linens.

*Time-of-Year Shower.* Assign each guest a month and have them bring gifts that reflect their designated months. This is also a good theme for decorations; you can decorate the tables in different seasons. Gift ideas include: February, lingerie; June, an iced-tea pitcher and tumblers; October, an afghan or wool blanket; December, a cappuccino maker and/or mugs.

*Seasonal Shower.* Same as the Time-of-Year Shower, but broken down by seasons—spring, summer, fall, winter.

*Hobby Shower.* Everyone brings gifts that reflect the couple's favorite hobbies or activities. If the couple is extremely active, gifts could range from one-year memberships at a health club to home free weights. Are they an outdoorsy kind of couple? Try camping stuff (such as tents, a hibachi, mess kits, and so on). A hammock can remind them to enjoy some quiet time together.

*Scrapbook Shower.* Along with miscellaneous gifts, guests bring either a scrap of something they shared with the bride—such as ticket stubs or an old picture—or a written anecdote about the bride. Everyone saves this kind of junk; some pretty wonderful stuff will turn up. During the shower, everyone pastes her scrap or anecdote into a scrapbook for the bride to keep.

*Recipe Shower.* Everyone brings, along with her gift, a favorite recipe. Collect them in a recipe file for the bride to keep. This can be done in conjunction with the Kitchen Shower.

*Invent some of your own!* Shower themes can be personalized to encompass anything, from the location of the honeymoon (a Hawaiian theme) to how the couple met (Gym theme). Decorate accordingly and you're off!

## SHOWER GAMES

Okay, so the guests have come from all corners of the state and even farther, lugging large, expensive gifts. Are you going to have them just sit around eating and *ooh*ing and *ahh*ing while the bride opens her gifts? Boring! That's why the bridal shower game was created—so that we can inject a little flavor into this redundant ritual and tease the bride at the same time, all in the name of good old-fashioned fun. Some ideas for shower games and activities include the following:

*The Bridal-Gown Game.* Hostesses provide lots of rolls of toilet paper. Guests get assigned to groups of four and each group gets one roll of toilet paper. Each group selects a model; they proceed to design a wedding gown and headpiece for her made out of toilet paper. No tape or glue is allowed. Then there is a fashion show and the bride chooses the best gown. Each person in that group wins a prize. (See the list of suggested prizes on page 48).

*The Clothespin Game.* This traditional game has been around forever. When each guest arrives, she gets a clothespin put on her sleeve. The guests are instructed that they are not allowed to cross their legs during the party. Whoever catches someone else crossing her legs gets the offender's clothespin. If that person has several clothespins, the person who caught her claims them all. The point is to collect as many as possible. The woman with the most pins at the end of the shower wins a prize.

*The Roast.* Guests are asked to come prepared with little pieces of poetry or anecdotes about the bride to read aloud at the shower. This game can get ugly, however.

*The Wedding-Night Game.* Another traditional game is for one of the bridesmaids to secretly write down each exclamation or remark made by the bride as she opens each gift. After all of the gifts are opened, the remarks are read to the guests as the things she is going to say on her wedding night. The responses range from "OOOOOO" and "AAAaaahhhh" to "I'm so excited" or "Oh, it's so beautiful." You get the point. Another twist on this inane, yet somehow pretty entertaining ritual is to add the words "under the sheets" after each remark. (Personally, we don't think this is as funny.)

*The Trivia Quiz.* Ahead of time, a sheet of questions about the couple, some of which are about things that can only be guessed, is prepared and copies are made. At the shower, the quiz sheets are distributed to the guests. Whoever answers the most questions correctly wins. Since the bride knows the answers, she is the judge. Here are some sample questions we think will get the party rolling:

1. Where did the bride and groom meet?
2. The groom is a _____ man.
    a) leg    b) breast    c) butt    d) other
3. What does the bride like best about the groom?
4. The couple's first date was where?
5. The couple's first trip together was to where?
6. What is the exact day the bride or groom proposed?
7. What is the groom's favorite activity or hobby?
8. What is the bride's favorite activity or hobby?
9. What kind of birth control does the couple use?
10. If the groom were a fruit, what would he be? Why?

Note: (Of course, the more shockable the guests—such as Great-gramma Flo and her 70-year-old spinster daughter—the tamer the questions should be.)

*Suggested prizes.* "Door prizes," as they are commonly known, are a great way to provide a little incentive and introduce some friendly competition into a shower game. They are also nice tokens of the shower for the victors and they don't have to be expensive. Try small picture frames, sachets, attractive note pads, atomizers, silver-plated bookmarks, a small plant, and so on.

# CHART FOR KEEPING TRACK OF GIFTS AND GIVERS

## BRIDAL SHOWER GIFTS
## TRACKING SHEET

| NAME | GIFT (BRIEF DESCRIPTION) | THANK-YOU SENT |
| --- | --- | --- |
| | | |
| | | |
| | | |
| | | |
| | | |
| | | |
| | | |
| | | |
| | | |
| | | |
| | | |
| | | |
| | | |
| | | |
| | | |
| | | |
| | | |
| | | |
| | | |
| | | |
| | | |
| | | |
| | | |

# BRIDAL SHOWER GIFTS
## TRACKING SHEET (CONTINUED)

| NAME | GIFT (BRIEF DESCRIPTION) | THANK-YOU SENT |
|------|--------------------------|----------------|
|      |                          |                |
|      |                          |                |
|      |                          |                |
|      |                          |                |
|      |                          |                |
|      |                          |                |
|      |                          |                |
|      |                          |                |
|      |                          |                |
|      |                          |                |
|      |                          |                |
|      |                          |                |
|      |                          |                |
|      |                          |                |
|      |                          |                |
|      |                          |                |
|      |                          |                |
|      |                          |                |
|      |                          |                |
|      |                          |                |
|      |                          |                |
|      |                          |                |
|      |                          |                |

# CHAPTER SIX
# Protocol/Etiquette

*[Etiquette is] a substitute for war.*

—ELBERT HUBBARD

IMAGINE YOURSELF at an elegant French restaurant with the handsome, smart guy you've been dating for several months. He's meeting your parents for the first time. Suddenly he picks up the flower vase, tosses the blooms, and replenishes his water glass with the contents of the vase. You're flabbergasted and horrified. You think, "Who is this guy? What other bizarre behavior will he treat me to if I stick around?"

Sometimes even the most intelligent and sensible people get a little nervous when the spotlight is on them. Combine scrutiny with flashbulbs and a finger bowl and suddenly they're acting as if they were raised in a barn. You laugh—but at a wedding, this could be you. One certain way to avoid socially short-circuiting and making a spectacle of yourself is to rely on your good breeding (or just follow our advice).

Growing up, you were taught everything you needed to know about table manners and how to be a charming weekend guest, but chances are your mother or other legal guardian let wedding etiquette slide. Now that the wedding invitations outnumber the J. Crew catalogs in your mailbox, you find yourself wondering if it's crass to give cash as a gift and whether it is acceptable to have a date accompany you. As a wedding guest, you can often get by on common sense and with some advice-seeking phone calls. But the day you receive The Call, the questions multiply and issues of dignity loom. Good wishes and a mail-order gift won't suffice. The time has come for a new level of professionalism. As a bridesmaid, you've got to do more than show up. You've got to behave.

A wedding is the bride and groom's Big Day, but all eyes are on the entire wedding party. A not-so-funny thing can happen when you put on a dress that's been picked out especially for you—and five other girls. You may feel a lot more like window dressing than the beloved friend the bride wanted to include in her wedding. Fears of resembling decoration understandably lead to feelings of vulnerability and anxiety. You may be seized with an urgency to assert your individuality. Perhaps you'll roar into the church parking lot on your Harley-Davidson while the bells are chiming, or nuzzle the priest on the dance floor, or pull out your harmonica and jam with the band. Forget it. Stand out by knowing the drill and performing it with grace. This is what breeding is about. It doesn't shout, it shows.

## THE WELL-MANNERED BRIDESMAID

*Manners adorn knowledge, and smooth its way through the world.*

—LORD CHESTERFIELD

Protocol? Etiquette? No, these are not concepts that became outmoded when Eisenhower left office. They are virtually synonymous. Protocol is a code, established by precedence. It is a rule that you can memorize and follow. Etiquette is the conduct prescribed by authority to be observed in social or official life. Etiquette and protocol are traditional rules of behavior established over generations. These social codes impose order on a complex world and remind people to interact honorably and with sensitivity. You learn etiquette at home, by watching and mimicking role models. You exercise etiquette—good manners—with the help of instinct, sound judgment, and your heart. The rules of etiquette may sometimes seem inflexible, but should be viewed as a helpful road map across unfamiliar territory, or simply the double yellow line on a road well traveled. As a blue-blooded race-car driver once observed, protocol tells you how to put the wheel on the axle, etiquette is the grease that makes the wheel spin, and good manners inspire the winner of the race to shake hands with the other drivers. Protocol tells you through which door to make an entrance; etiquette tells you how and to whom you introduce yourself once you are inside. The warmth of your introduction and the personalized gift you thought to bring are the admirable manners that get you invited back. Get it? Protocol and etiquette can be diagrammed; manners makes elegant use of the diagram, doesn't flaunt the diagram, and never embarrasses others who don't have it. Traditions change, but what follows are some protocol basics for bridesmaids to remember, along with ABCs that distinguish well-mannered bridesmaids from the ill-mannered.

1. The prospective bridesmaid responds to the bride's invitation to be a member of the wedding party if not immediately, as promptly as possible. As soon as she has a wedding date in mind, the bride is obligated to inform as many family members and close friends as she can, so no one feels slighted by hearing the exciting news secondhand. When the bride makes these calls, she asks some individuals to be attendants. Therefore, help her out by giving her an answer as quickly as you can.

   ✢ *An assenting bridesmaid first asks the bride to give her an estimation of the costs involved and has checked her bank account to ensure it can withstand the financial burden of the mission.*

   ✢ *The ambitious prospective bridesmaid inquires about the number of single men who will be at the wedding before confirming that she can participate.*

2. The bridesmaid is not expected to respond to the wedding invitation she receives. As she has agreed to be a bridesmaid, it is understood that she will be at the wedding. The invitation is sent to be kept as a memento.

❧ *A beloved bridesmaid includes the invitation at the end of a personalized scrapbook she presents to the bride at the shower.*

⚥ *The battle-weary bridesmaid throws the invitation into a drawer with her diaphragm, her condoms, and the fifteen other wedding invitations that have arrived in the mail this year.*

3. Bridesmaids pay for their own dresses, accessories, and travel expenses. The bride should make lodging available for out-of-town attendants with nearby relatives and friends, and arrange for group rates at a local hotel. If a bridesmaid prefers to stay at the local hotel, she is responsible for her bill.

   A generous bride may help her bridesmaid with some of these expenses. If the bride's maiden name is Hilton or Marriott, her attendants ought to concern themselves with room service rather than room rates.

❧ *A cost-conscious bridesmaid cheerfully accepts the accommodations at Aunt Dora's home and sleeps in a bunk bed.*

⚥ *The cheap bridesmaid totals her expenses and deducts this sum from the price of what she will spend on the wedding gift.*

4. Bridesmaids wear the dress the bride has chosen for her wedding attendants. Ideally, the bride has selected three styles from which her attendants can chose.

❧ *A diplomatic bridesmaid sensibly steers the bride toward an attractive dress that is affordable for all attendants.*

⚥ *The determined bridesmaid insists on the dress that is most flattering to her figure; the wedding is her opportunity to meet her future husband.*

5. Bridesmaids assure the bride that the dress they must wear is a vision of couture, especially when compared to other bridesmaid dresses they've seen or had to wear previously.

❧ *An economical bridesmaid already knows the name of the consignment shop that will resell the dress for her.*

🍃 *The environmentally conscious bridesmaid recycles the gown as a scarecrow for her vegetable garden and forgets to remove it before the bride comes over for tea after her honeymoon.*

6. Bridesmaids organize and pay for the bridal shower.

   🍂 *A frugal bridesmaid comparison-shops for the caterer that will give them the biggest bang for their buck.*

   🍃 *The forgetful bridesmaid never booked the private room at the restaurant where the shower is being held.*

7. Bridesmaids defer to the maid of honor in matters of planning the bridal shower.

   🍂 *A gracious bridesmaid offers useful suggestions about place, theme, and guest list.*

   🍃 *The grudging bridesmaid shows up late to indicate her displeasure with the early hour set for the shower, and spikes the punch because nobody else wanted mimosas.*

8. Bridesmaids cooperate with each other.

   🍂 *A harmonious bridesmaid exchanges her phone number with the other attendants and goes with the flow.*

   🍃 *The halfhearted bridesmaid doesn't know the names of her comrades. The hell-bent bridesmaid treats every detail as a matter of life and death.*

9. Bridesmaids assist the bride with wedding-related errands and, if the bride is not having a calligrapher address her invitations, may help address them by hand.

   🍂 *An indefatigable bridesmaid offers to pick up the helium tank for the reception party balloons with her Ford Explorer when she hears that all the ushers drive Miatas.*

   🍃 *The inept bridesmaid takes her car to the repair shop the week before the wedding, owns a broken answering machine, and leaves traces of her lipstick on each envelope that she seals.*

10. Bridesmaids participate in all pre-wedding parties and wedding-related functions. These may include an engagement party, the bridal shower, a luncheon for the bridesmaids, a rehearsal dinner, and a breakfast the morning after the wedding.

   *❧ A joyful bridesmaid is always punctual and ready with a camera to record those special moments.*

   *❦ The jealous bridesmaid is available only for the wedding ceremony, or attends only some of the functions, making it amply clear to all other participants the many appointments she had to juggle to make her presence possible. She, not the bride, is the star.*

11. Bridesmaids entertain the bride on the night when the groom is at his bachelor's party.

   *❧ A kindly bridesmaid arranges a lovely dinner for the bride at her favorite restaurant.*

   *❦ The kinky bridesmaid pays a gorgeous fireman to show up at the bride's door after her lovely dinner.*

12. Bridesmaids assuage the bride's last-minute misgivings about her future husband.

   *❧ A loyal bridesmaid tells the bride that her jitters are natural.*

   *❦ The lethal bridesmaid reveals rumors she's heard about the groom's infidelities.*

13. Bridesmaids arrive at the dressing site two hours before the ceremony and assist the bride with her gown and grooming preparation.

   *❧ A meticulous bridesmaid arranges a carpool with other attendants and brings a survival kit with extra stockings, clear nail polish, and other necessities.*

   *❦ The messy bridesmaid shows up late with her dog in tow.*

14. Bridesmaids sign the wedding guest book.

   ❧ *A noteworthy bridesmaid neatly signs her name and records a personal remark that the bride will always treasure.*

   ❦ *The nosy bridesmaid flips through the book and reads everyone else's entry while other guests wait to add their own names and good wishes.*

15. Bridesmaids arrive dressed at the ceremony site one hour before the wedding for photographs.

   ❧ *An optimistic bridesmaid smiles charmingly on command so the session doesn't last two hours.*

   ❦ *The obnoxious bridesmaid wears false eyelashes that flutter in the breeze and perfume that makes everyone sneeze.*

16. Bridesmaids walk behind ushers in order of height during the processional, either in pairs or in single file.

   ❧ *A poised bridesmaid stands straight and smiles without fail.*

   ❦ *The political bridesmaid refuses to walk behind an usher and carries her bouquet like a firearm.*

17. Bridesmaids stand to the left of the maid of honor and slightly behind her during the ceremony, facing the officiant.

   ❧ *A qualified bridesmaid knows to be quiet while she listens to the cherished words that the bride and groom exchange during the ceremony.*

   ❦ *The quixotic bridesmaid recites the vows that she would have written.*

18. Bridesmaids are escorted out by the ushers (to each usher's right) immediately following the maid of honor and the best man during the recessional.

&#x261E; *A reasonable bridesmaid adjusts her pace to that of the couple in front of her and trusts that her escort will do the same.*

&#x260F; *The reproachful bridesmaid trips herself on the dress she didn't want to pay a tailor to hem and hisses at her companion to slow down.*

19. Bridesmaids stand to the left of the maid of honor in the receiving line (optional). Check with the bride; she may ask that her bridesmaids circulate among the guests instead.

&#x261E; *A sociable bridesmaid greets each guest with warm words of welcome.*

&#x260F; *The shocking bridesmaid offers guests unsolicited comments about the suitability of the nuptial match and, while gulping from her glass, apologizes that the champagne is Californian and not French.*

20. Bridesmaids compliment the mother of the bride on how youthful she looks.

&#x261E; *A thoughtful bridesmaid opines that the mother of the bride can still fit into the gown she wore on her wedding day.*

&#x260F; *The toxic bridesmaid asks her who does her collagen injections.*

21. Bridesmaids sit next to the ushers at the head table in alternating seats. At the head table where the wedding party is seated, there should be place cards.

&#x261E; *An understanding bridesmaid does not tap her glass incessantly with her silverware, demanding that the bride and groom kiss for the crowd.*

&#x260F; *The unrestrained bridesmaid switches placecards so she is seated next to the sexiest usher, then removes the satin ribbon from her napkin and ties the usher's wrist to his chair.*

22. Bridesmaids do not react inappropriately to sentimental toasts.

☙ *A vigilant bridesmaid never yawns while the father of the bride drones on nostalgically about his little girl who has grown up.*

𝒫 *The vampish bridesmaid winks at the groom as he toasts his new wife.*

23. Bridesmaids may offer a toast, but only after the best man's toast, the groom's toast to his bride, and words from the bride, parents, and relatives.

   ☙ *A witty bridesmaid composes a clever and short poem to wish the bride and groom a loving and prosperous future together.*

   𝒫 *The wanton bridesmaid reveals that she and the groom played Spin the Bottle in junior high and that she hopes his technique has improved since then.*

24. Bridesmaids dance with ushers and other important guests.

   ☙ *A Xenon dance-clubbing bridesmaid foxtrots with the bride's groping fifteen-year-old brother, makes the bride's grandfather feel like Fred Astaire, and comes equipped with a pair of rubber-soled flats.*

   𝒫 *The xenophobic bridesmaid refuses to dance with men she doesn't know. The X-rated bridesmaid wants to lambada stripped down to her black leather G-string.*

25. Bridesmaids tell the bride repeatedly that she has never looked so radiant and everything is perfect.

   ☙ *A yielding bridesmaid allows the bride to be the center of attention.*

   𝒫 *The yearning bridesmaid asks, "What about me?"*

26. Bridesmaids circulate among the guests and act as deputy hostesses.

   ☙ *A zealous bridesmaid makes a point of engaging any guest who is standing alone in light, friendly conversation and setting him or her at ease.*

   𝒫 *The Zen bridesmaid sits quietly by herself meditating.*

27. Bridesmaids encourage single women to participate in the bouquet-tossing ceremony. This usually takes place in the last half hour of the reception.

    &#x273D; *An altruistic bridesmaid allows charity cases optimum catch position.*

    &#x1F53E; *The aggressive bridesmaid body-checks any female over fifteen who gets between her and a fistful of flying lilies.*

28. Like any other guest, the bridesmaid has a year to give the couple a wedding present.

    &#x273D; *Sometimes, it makes sense to wait a year. If the couple is buying a new home, they'll appreciate receiving gifts at their new address. A bullish bridesmaid buys the newlyweds four place settings, anticipating the needs of a young family.*

    &#x1F53E; *Sometimes, it makes sense to wait a year. You never know— what do you think their chances are? The bookie bridesmaid calculates the couple's odds of staying together and indiscreetly collects for the pot.*

Having a grasp of wedding etiquette is essential to your survival as a bridesmaid. The bridesmaid of good character understands that her performance speaks volumes about her respect and love for the bride. She'll use these guidelines to express her awareness about the bride's special concerns and needs at this tumultuous time, and to complete her mission with grace and ease. When in doubt, assess the circumstances, and refer to the codes you have memorized. Decide upon the most common-sensical and kind solution, take action, and keep a sense of humor. No matter how intimidated you are by the shifting moods of the bride or the demands of her tyrannical mother, you'll breathe easier knowing that there are certain unchanging rules with which you've armed yourself before entering the strange and chaotic world they've constructed, which probably feels like a jungle.

*Good manners are made up of petty sacrifices.*

—RALPH WALDO EMERSON

When a friend asks you to be her bridesmaid, realize that she's creating a fantasy and you're invited to join it. Remember when you were very young and played "pretend"? The neighborhood kid with the dominant personality (the bully) got to set the rules. Now you're an adult and the bride is the dominant personality, a princess who will be transformed into a queen during this play. Remember that it's already been established that she gets the hero, so the only way to win this game is to look noble while helping her achieve that perfect day. What if she grossly oversteps all boundaries of friendship and propriety? Why, set her straight. Of course, you'll try diplomacy before guerrilla tactics. Read on.

## QUESTIONS AND ANSWERS

Q: I love my cousin dearly, but for her wedding, which is on Halloween, she has chosen orange bridesmaid dresses and green hats. We are supposed to carry a candle instead of flowers. I refuse to be dressed as a pumpkin!

—Spooked in Spokane

A: Dear Spooked,

Not only does this witch expect you to dress like a pumpkin, she's asking you to pay for the privilege. Unless she is planning a very campy wedding—that is, if the officiant is Dracula and the groom is going to bite the bride's neck—this costume is inappropriate for a traditional wedding. Alas, you cannot drop out because you hate the dress. If that were permitted, bridesmaids would be extinct.

Enlist the help of her mother and your own to exert subtle familial pressure. Invite the other bridesmaids to your house or schedule a conference call to discuss the regalia. If the other women concur that this attire is hideous, contact the bride and let her know that you all feel uncomfortable. If she still refuses to acquiesce, you've got to remember that this wedding is her dream, and the color and style of dress are a reflection of her taste, not your own. Don't ridicule her and make her feel like a fool. Bite the bullet, wear the dress, and laugh about it later.

Guerrilla tactics we would never recommend: If she insists and the attendants find themselves being fitted in orange tents at the bridal salon, pay an elegant stranger to whisper audibly:"Some brides try so hard to be original, it's just tacky." The elegant stranger's chic friend must murmur, "Yes, it is so sad." If all else fails and you must endure this indignity, don't throw rice at her after the Halloween ceremony. Throw pumpkin seeds.

Q: A good friend has just asked me to be her bridesmaid. Her wedding, to which I was invited, is next week. She told me I am replacing another friend who had to cancel because of an emergency. I feel insulted to be asked to be a member of the wedding party so late. How should I respond?

—Polly Proxy

A: Dear Ms. Polly,
You've been chosen! Forget grievances about being a "second-best" friend and accept. You say the bride is a good friend; welcome this milestone in your relationship, roll up your sleeves and you'll become an even better friend. However, if you're no Pollyanna and can't shake off the feeling that you're just a convenient stand in, go directly to Chapter Twelve, "Just Say No." Better to be a cheerful guest than a churlish attendant.

Q: I've been a bridesmaid ten times and, unlike most women I know, I love the entire zany process! A co-worker recently asked if I'd be her bridesmaid. Of course, I accepted in a heartbeat, but now my worry is this: Am I obligated to ask each woman for whom I've been a bridesmaid to be my bridesmaid when I get married? If so, I am going to have to say no to this woman and everyone else until after I've had my own ceremony.

—Madcap Martyr

A: Dear Madcap Martyr,
You are truly one in a million. Doubtless many will be disappointed that they cannot march for you on your triumphant day, but fortunately you are not required to

reciprocate the favor of asking someone to be your bridesmaid. Carry on!

Q: Along with five other bridesmaids, I am planning a shower for a bride who is insisting that we invite her father, brothers and fiancé. We are livid, as we had planned an afternoon tea, and everyone knows that men won't eat finger sandwiches. We are all busy professionals and don't want to scrap our original plans. How do we satisfy her?

—Teed off in Boston

A: Dear Boston Tea Party,
I daresay that a bride who wants so many males present at such a traditionally female gathering would herself not fully appreciate the pleasures of a tea. If the wedding date allows, throw her shower on Super Bowl Sunday. Either the men won't come at all, or they will come with their own beer and pizza. She can explore both her yin and yang sides as you and the other bridesmaids share scones and lovely Devonshire cream. Remember, this is the one wedding event other than the bachelor party in which *the bride has no say!* The guest list, activities, and food are at the sole discretion of you and your fellow bridesmaids, who don't have to plan this nice occasion for the bride at all. Pass along this information to your rude bride. You don't have to satisfy her. That's the groom's job.

Q: I am my sister's maid of honor and want to plan her bridal shower, but I have read that the bride's relatives are not supposed to give the shower. Why not? How can I proceed without appearing gauche?

—Feeling Greedy

A: Dear Feeling Greedy,
Traditionally, members of the immediate family are not supposed to give the bridal shower, as it would appear unseemly to solicit gifts for a sister or daughter. However, it is the maid of honor who is officially responsible for the shower, and it is perfectly acceptable for a sister to be the maid of honor. The way out of this quandary is to ask an enthusiastic bridesmaid to be your co-coordinator and mail the invitations under her name.

Q: I am a maid of honor trying to plan a shower for a bride whose mother is already warring with the groom's mother over wedding arrangements. Each has offered to pay for all the shower expenses and has very specific ideas about the kind of shower I should give. How do I handle them?

—The Ref

A: Dear Ms. Ref,

Advise these dueling dowagers that as the maid of honor, you are the general in charge of this congenial function. You can give the bride a wonderful shower on a limited budget (see Chapter Five, "The Bridal Shower") that allows you and the other bridesmaids to foot the bill. These women had their chance to serve at least three decades ago.

Accept their money only if they agree to follow your orders. If only for one day, they must be allies. Warn them that your primary goal is to make the bride happy at her shower. If they break their peace treaty, they cannot sit down at the table.

Q: The bride never asked me whether I'd be bringing a date to the wedding. Shall I tell her first, or can I just show up with him?

—Lucky in Love

A: Dear Lucky,

Refrain from surprising the bride, other than with a bridal shower. Ask her if you can bring an escort (see "Your Date," p. 91). Usually, a wedding invitation extends to a spouse or significant other. If she allows you to bring your Romeo, take the quiz on p. 93 before you tell him the good news.

Q: As a bridesmaid, I helped plan and attended one shower for the bride. Now her co-workers have asked me to one that they are giving. Must I go and do I have to buy a second gift?

—Broke in Brooklyn

A: Dear Broke,

It would be nice if you went and met these other friends of the bride, but you do not have to bring a second shower gift. This would be excessive. In addition to the bridal attendants, family friends, colleagues and distant relatives may want to give showers. If several people want to give the bride a shower, they should consult with the bride so she can help divide the guest lists. The shower should be a pleasantly anticipated event, rather than a burden, so nobody should be invited to more than two.

Q: I am the matron of honor for a bride who has been married once before. What kind of shower is suitable?

—Sticky Situation

A: Dear Sticky,
Ask the bride what she wants. She may feel uncomfortable asking friends who participated in her first shower to come to a second, bearing more gifts. Consider a small luncheon. Lavish gifts would be inappropriate and standard housewarming gifts are probably unnecessary.

Q: I've already purchased and paid for the bridesmaid dress that the bride originally selected for her wedding. She has since fallen in love with a new dress and has asked all the bridesmaids to buy this dress also. What can I do?

—Friends with Flaky

A: Dear Friend,
A bride must be compassionate. Her fickleness should not strain your finances. Even if all her bridesmaids can afford another dress, it is wrong. Take her aside and tell her that your budget for her wedding does not allow for a second dress. Unless she wants to pay for this dress, regretfully state that you are going to have to drop out of the wedding party.

Q: I am Jewish and will be a bridesmaid at my friend's Catholic wedding. Am I supposed to participate in the religious part of the ceremony?

—Clueless in Cleveland

A: Dear Clueless,
Yes, the attendants are supposed to take part in the ceremony, even if the attendant belongs to another faith. You may not take communion or drink from the chalice, but you should join in the prayer and kneel, stand, kneel, stand with all the other guests in the church.

Q: The bride and groom are both recently graduated students. I'd like to give them cash, but heard that this is not appropriate as a wedding present. Can I break the rules?

—Practical in Poughkeepsie

A: Dear Practical,
The argument against cash has always been that it is wrong for the bride and groom to know the monetary value of your gift. Well, don't they also know the dollar amount for every item for which they've registered? We dismiss this etiquette rule as outdated and say that money is a practical, always happily accepted gift; has it ever been exchanged because it was the wrong color?

Q: I saw a crystal vase that I would like to buy for the bride and groom, but it was at a store where they are not registered. The bride grows roses and I think this vase would look spectacular in their new home. Can I still buy it for them?

—Dream Guest

A: Dear Guest,
Yes. The best gifts are the ones chosen with care and given with love in your heart. This sounds like that kind of gift.

Being a bridesmaid can strain a friendship, or it can bring two friends closer together. At times your duties will feel anachronistic, but there is nothing old-fashioned about supporting a friend. Who needs etiquette and good manners? We all do. They are the basis for wonderful friendships that reward you with comfort and happiness all your life—including the day you get to enact your own long-held wedding fantasy!

## ANECDOTES

### The Good

- A Connecticut bride eloped at the last minute, exasperated by the bickering between her mother and the groom's mother over the wedding plans. She made arrangements with the bridal boutique to buy back her attendant's gowns and then sent them each a bouquet of tea roses—the flowers they were supposed to hold during the ceremony.

- A New Jersey bride planned a very extravagant wedding complete with haute couture bridesmaid gowns, recognized the economic burden she had placed on one of her less financially able bridesmaids, and discreetly offered to cover part of her expenses. The offer was gratefully accepted.
- A reluctant bridesmaid from Los Angeles gave up her Fourth of July weekend to fly to Houston for her college roommate's wedding. At the rehearsal dinner she was seated next to an usher who was also from Los Angeles. Fireworks ensued and they were married two years later during the Fourth of July weekend in their own city.
- One Manhattan bridesmaid, short on cash from living in the fast lane, was able to negotiate a lay-a-way plan with the sympathetic store owner with whom the bride made arrangements for the bridesmaids' gowns. This arrangement made it possible for her to proudly fulfill her bridesmaid's duties *and* pay Con Ed.
- A young single rabbi was asked to perform the marriage ceremony for one of the couples in his congregation. At the wedding, the father of the bride invited the Rabbi to stay for the reception and introduced him to his other daughter—the maid of honor. A match was made and they were married the next year!
- After catching her third consecutive bouquet at a friend's wedding, a frustrated Philadelphia bridesmaid vowed never to participate in the useless ritual again. Later that year, as a bridesmaid in a college roommate's wedding, she was cajoled into participating in the dreaded toss. Once again, she was victorious. She cringed at the idea of having to endure some lout placing the garter on her leg and watched the garter toss in agony. The winner? The groom's handsome roommate from Yale law school. As he moved the garter up her thigh, her body temperature rose. The two were married within the year.

## The Bad

- In Manhattan, a maid of honor who was trying to plan a shower with the bride's future sister-in-law became incensed when the relative never returned any of her phone calls. She ultimately mailed out the shower invitations without listing the girl's name alongside her own for the R.S.V.P. The groom called her to complain and told her to apologize to his sister.

- During a postceremony photo session, a gushing Michigan bridesmaid holding a glass of wine went to congratulate the bride. An excited guest ran up behind her, and threw his arms out to embrace them both. He knocked the wine all over the front of the bride's gown—before she even had a chance to greet any of her guests! The moral? Always serve white wine at a wedding reception.
- After the processional to the *chupah* at a Boston wedding, one matron of honor took it upon herself to entertain the guests during the ceremony with a Charleston jig. She was ostracized during the reception.
- A Southern bridesmaid visiting up North didn't understand the nickname "Denise the Menace" given to a sweet-looking, towheaded flower girl. During pictures before the ceremony, when the visiting bridesmaid was asked to hold the flower girl, the child bit her.
- One Dallas bride arranged for a hairdresser to come to her hotel room and do both her and her bridesmaids' hair. A selfish bridesmaid was unhappy with her coif and insisted that the hairdresser style her hair again and again until she was satisfied. The bride was still waiting her turn. Eventually, the bride had to do her own hair.
- A Miami bridesmaid was asked to wear a bright banana-yellow dress, and was told at the rehearsal that the processional would consist of *dancing* down the aisle, in a traditional ethnic ceremony. (And you were worried *you'd* slip . . . )

### And the Ugly

- A bewildered Rhode Island bridesmaid was stranded on the dance floor in the middle of the first waltz when her partner, the usher who had escorted her down the aisle, was hauled away by his 300-pound date as she hissed that he'd been "too willing."
- One New York bridesmaid didn't leave enough time to drive to a wedding in Boston. She got stuck in traffic and arrived five minutes before she was due for pictures. Having planned

to primp at the hotel, she ultimately had to go to the wedding unshowered!

- A Kentucky bride received a cocker spaniel puppy from her groom. She asked her maid of honor to hold "Cupcake" while she had her hair done. The dog wet on the maid of honor's gown. The bride laughed and commented that the dog was as nervous as his mistress. As for the urine-soaked gown, she joked, "Well, the show must go on!"

- During a bouquet toss at a Boston wedding, a group of young unmarried women eagerly awaited the pitch. When the bouquet was thrown, a sixtyish woman who had been through a recent bitter divorce dashed in front of the maidens, snatched the bouquet, and shouted, "I need this more than you!"

- One New York City maid of honor, the sister of the bride, organized a surprise engagement party at a renowned hotel and informed guests it would be a cash bar. Appropriately, she wrote "no gifts" on the invitation, then called certain friends of the bride to tell them that the "no gifts" request didn't apply to them, and they *really* shouldn't come "empty-handed."

# CHAPTER SEVEN

# The Bachelorette Party

THE MOST successful covert operations take place under cover of night. Measures of success include: the target subject has been brainwashed with the appropriate propaganda; an environment has been plundered; booty is recovered; that these activities have not been captured on film; and all soldiers return home safely.

Bachelor parties are infamous for providing the groom with his last hurrah as a free man. Typically this party involves interaction with members of the opposite sex. As no self-respecting female would want to be any man's toy for one night, let alone a soon-to-be-married man surrounded by his lecherous pals, the women are usually of the bored, hired variety—strippers, hookers, exotic dancers at topless bars and so on. Although the groom pretends to relish the prospect of a sordid night out with his rowdy chug-a-lug buddies, it was one too many of these nights that sent him to Tiffany's engagement-ring counter in the first place. Most men come home from this primitive rite of passage relieved that it is over and convinced that their single friends' personal lives are pathetic. A lot more drinking goes on than real sweaty action.

## WHY NOT?

So why should the guys have all the fun? Especially when, as in most things, women can do it better. Whether you choose port and cigars over damask-covered tables, or tequila and dancing *on* the tables, treat yourself to a girls' night out. A bachelorette party for the bride can recreate those bar-hopping nights during which you had to fend off men after accepting the drinks they bought and the days spent gossiping about the professional basketball player Cheryl made out with in a banquette. As the bride's mother is usually at the bridal shower, the bachelorette party is the ideal time to give the bride the sexy lingerie she'd rather not display in front of her mother and to reminisce about past boyfriends. All sorts of venues are available and can make for a memorable nighttime or weekend getaway.

## PARTY IDEAS

1. **A new trendy restaurant.** This is a great, harmless place to play eye hockey with handsome men and flex your flirtation muscles while looking your best.
2. **A favorite restaurant.** If the group has a tried-and-true hangout, why not go there? Order artery-clogging foods that the health-conscious groom won't allow the bride to ingest, like cheeseburgers and fries. Wash it down with plenty of cheap beer and then pick out names for the next generation.
3. **A weekend getaway at a spa.** If you can afford it, this is really the luxurious weekend you'll want to make a tradition. Gretchen in the white coat will knead the tension knots out of the bride's neck and Lya will repair the bridal party's chewed fingernails. Pear salads and eucalyptus steam baths for everyone!
4. **A weekend at a beach house or ski resort condo.** Before she takes the big final step, the bride will appreciate the beach for long walks or the fresh air of an alpine mountain to clear her head. Rum is the preferred all-weather drink, whether mixed with Coke or hot buttered, and an excellent catalyst for mischief. Throw some Jimmy Buffett CDs into your duffel bag.
5. **Disco night.** Break out the satin and the platform shoes for a feverish night with the Bee Gees, the Bay City Rollers, and the Icon of Love, Barry White. The bride can bury her face

in a hairy chest under a multifaceted globe and come home with serpentine gold chain indentations on her cheek.

6. **A cultural field trip.** The bride loves Seurat; the groom is a contractor who would rather watch paint dry than contemplate the chromo-luminism of *A Sunday Afternoon on the Island of La Grande Jatte.* Treat her to tickets for the most exciting museum show of the year in New York, Philadelphia, or Boston.

7. **Brunch with the body builders.** After Bloody Marys and eggs Benedict, take a road trip to watch men you'd never dream of marrying flex their biceps and twist their slick torsos at an out-of-state competition. Ask if you can feel their muscles. All of them.

8. **A wine tasting.** Occasionally vineyards hold wine-tasting nights, as do some restaurants. Under the starlit skies, sit at a picnic table with congenial strangers and sample the five main categories of wine. Start with a Bordeaux, sip from your neighbor's Meursault and reach for the Zinfandel. The food is an afterthought.

9. **A cowboy bar.** Go to the real ones where the men know how to line dance. Feel the reverberations of the sawdust floor as 50 couples kick up their boot heels. Feel your heart pound as Marlboro Man pulls you closer with callused hands. He rustles steer during the day and the pickup truck is parked just outside. He's called "Tex," and you never ask for a last name.

   And then there's . . .

10. **The strip joint.** Find an imaginative skin show that features men in uniform—doctor, lawyer, Indian chief—who take it all off. Peel a Ulysses S. Grant from a wad of bills and hand it to the bride to stick in a mustachioed policeman's holster. You know all these cheesy men are gay, but it's fun to watch their naked bodies gyrate and to shout, "Wag it!" The flower girl stays home.

It's usually wise to make this outing a couple of weeks before the wedding. Allow the bride time to recover from her night of reckless debauchery. Dark undereye circles diminish in two days. Bruised lips take longer. Throw her bachelorette party on the night the groom plays stupid drinking games with his ushers. You'll distract her from worrying about Fred hurting himself, and imagine how he'll feel when he climbs into bed at 3:00 A.M., calls Betsy, and gets no answer. If they are already cohabitating, he'll pace until she bursts in the front door at 7:00 A.M., whistling Joe Cocker's "Feeling Alright." He'll comprehend that his future wife's friends know how to show her a better time than his own friends do him, and that she can handle it. He'll respect their *joie de vivre* and never extend a business trip.

# CHAPTER EIGHT

# The Wedding Rehearsal and the Rehearsal Dinner

A MOCK battle or simulated skirmish introduces the soldiers to battle-like conditions so that they can troubleshoot before the actual, high-stakes occurrence.

## THE REHEARSAL

Like any theatrical event, rehearsals are crucial for a successful show. We all know a wedding is one big Broadway extravaganza: boy lead, girl lead, boy meets girl, they fall in love, they kiss, they're married. There's music playing, people singing, and assigned seating. There's even a big dance number; it's called The Processional. (Right together, left together, right together, left together, stop, and turn . . . ) Well, the wedding rehearsal is just a dress rehearsal without the fancy costumes. This is your opportunity to iron out all of the kinks in the program before the big show. You'll be performing live and you'll be subject to intense scrutiny. Perform beautifully, and you'll receive raves, maybe even applause; stumble, and the reviews will haunt you until the day you die. Without a rehearsal, who knows what kind of mayhem might break out at the wedding: bridesmaids wandering aimlessly around the altar or *chupah*, like lost souls, wondering where they're supposed to stand; ushers racing down the aisle after the ceremony, leaving their designated bridesmaids behind. The rehearsal gives everyone in the wedding party an opportunity to go through the motions so that on the big day, when the director (a.k.a. the officiant) says "Places!", all the actors know where their places are. Traditionally done the night before the wedding, the point of the rehearsal is to give the whole bridal party a chance to "rehearse" the ceremony. A day or two before W-Day, the wedding party, the officiant, the musicians for the ceremony, and any other people participating in the ceremony (such as honored guests who might be reading a passage during the ceremony, flower children and so on) meet at the ceremony site to go through the motions. It is possible, particularly if the ceremony will not be in a church or synagogue, that the rehearsal will be just for the wedding party. It is also possible that the bride may choose not to rehearse, which may be all fine and dandy if the wedding will take place on a farm and the bridal party will be dressed in overalls. However, if the wedding is expected to be relatively traditional (for example, if guests will eat their meal with utensils and are expected to wear footwear), try to persuade the bride to have some form of rehearsal, even if it is extremely brief.

Weddings consist of three acts: the processional, the ceremony, and the recessional. It's important to know your place in each so that you can concentrate on trying to not to trip on the runner instead of wondering what you're supposed to do once you get to the end of the aisle. During the rehearsal, the wedding party practices the processional and the recessional and takes note of their positions for the ceremony. This is your only opportunity to practice your part, so be a good bridesmaid and try to pay attention.

## The Processional

The processional as we know it today is actually a drastically abbreviated version of the first wedding processionals. While in our society the processional refers to the bridal party's walk down the aisle and up to the *chupah* or altar, it is a mere vestige of the original processional. In past centuries, whole villages marched through town from the bride's home to either the new home or the church. Some villages in countries around the world still perform this processional ritual. But, chances are the whole town isn't invited to *your* wedding, and the people who *are* invited most likely won't be participating in a march through town, so it is safe to say that you can probably find your place in one of the standard processional formations listed in this section.

There are as many different styles of processionals as there are religions (including atheism) and it's important to know where you stand in each. Following are the most common processionals; please note your position in each.

PROTESTANT
In a Protestant procession, the officiant, the groom, and his best man are not a part of the procession. They are already positioned at the end of the aisle by the altar.

**First—Ushers.** Ushers enter from the back of the church in pairs, by height from shortest first to tallest last. If there is an odd number of ushers, the shortest usher should go down the aisle first. Spacing between each pair should be three to four pews.

**Second—Bridesmaids.** The bridesmaids follow right behind the ushers. If there are fewer than four bridesmaids, they should walk single file. While technically bridesmaids are not placed in order of importance during the processional, it is traditional that in the case where there are fewer than four bridesmaids, the bridesmaid who had the most responsibilities is at the back of this line, closest to the maid of honor. If the responsibilities were shared equally, the bridesmaids form a line according to height, with the most petite in front. Again, if there is an odd number of bridesmaids, the shortest goes first, by herself. More than four should pair off according to height. If there are **junior bridesmaids,** they follow the bridesmaids down the aisle, solo, in order of height.

**Third—The maid of honor.** The maid of honor follows the bridesmaids, or the junior bridesmaids if there are any. If there is a matron of honor as well, or two maids of honor, or two matrons of honor (or whatever!), they can walk down the aisle side-by-side or single file. It's the bride's choice.

**Fourth—The ring bearer and flower girl.** These young attendants follow the maid of honor. They can walk together or separately. In the case of the latter, the ring bearer goes first, and the flower girl goes right before the bride. While these young cherubs add charm to any ceremony, you may want to warn the bride about including extremely young children (under the age of two-and-a-half). We heard of an eighteen-month-old flower girl on her way down the aisle who announced to the guests that she had just gone "doo-doo". While some people think this is cute and adds a personal flair to the ceremony, not all brides are keen on diaper talk during a beautiful ceremony.

**Fifth—The bride and her father.** "Here comes the bride . . ." The bride is always on the left arm of her father.

CATHOLIC

A Catholic processional is the same as a Protestant processional, with the option that the ushers may also already be stationed at the end of the aisle with the officiant, the groom, and the best man.

JEWISH

At a Jewish wedding, everyone in the wedding party, including the officiant and both the bride's and groom's immediate families, is usually a part of the processional. Although there are variations on the positioning of the bridal party in the Jewish processional depending on whether the ceremony is Orthodox, Conservative, or Reform, the common processional is as follows:

**First—The rabbi.** The rabbi is first to walk down the aisle. If there is a cantor, he walks alongside the rabbi, on his right side.

**Second—The bride's grandparents.** "Bubbe" and "Zayde," as the bride affectionately calls them, follow the rabbi.

**Third—The groom's grandparents.** This proud couple follows the bride's grandparents, a position from which Grandma Goldberg can check out Grandma Weinstein's gown and comment to her husband on the tackiness of wearing beading in the afternoon.

**Fourth—Ushers and bridesmaids.** Marching in pairs of twos made up of one usher and one bridesmaid, these couples proceed down the aisle together in order of height—shortest first, tallest last. Of course, if there are more bridesmaids than ushers, an usher may escort two bridesmaids down the aisle at once. This coed pairing can probably be traced back to a shrewd matchmaker in a long-ago *shtetl*. No self-respecting Yenta would ever pass up an opportunity to introduce a nice Jewish boy to a nice Jewish girl.

**Fifth—The best man.**

**Sixth—The groom and his parents.** In the Jewish procession, the groom is always escorted by his parents, with his father on his left and his mother on his right.

**Seventh—The maid of honor.** As in a Christian ceremony, if there are two honor attendants, they can walk either side-by-side or single file, with the honor attendant who has performed the most duties just before the bride.

**Eighth—The ring bearer.** The ring bearer follows the maid of honor and marches down the aisle solo.

**Ninth—The flower girl.** Like the ring bearer, the flower girl also marches down the aisle solo. See the outline of the Protestant processional for our caveat.

**Tenth—The bride, her father, and her mother.** Enter the main attraction. As with the groom, the bride is escorted by both parents; her father is on her left, her mother on her right.

An alternative processional for a Jewish wedding is that the ushers walk down the aisle separately from the bridesmaids. When this processional is used, the ushers walk after both sets of grandparents and before the best man. Still another kind of procession is found in Orthodox Jewish weddings, where the wedding procession does not include ushers.

## CIVIL CEREMONY

This is where an on-site wedding coordinator comes in handy. Whether the wedding is at a large hotel or a small restaurant, there is a person in charge at the site who will know what type of procession best suits the site. Follow his or her lead.

## The Ceremony

Rehearsing the ceremony is almost as critical as rehearsing the processional. Everyone has an assigned place and you need to know where that place is (see "He Does, She Does" in Chapter

Nine). Also, it is very important that anyone who has a special role in the ceremony has a chance to run through his or her part at least once. This will give everyone an opportunity to see how the ceremony is going to flow and to pick up their cues (such as when the maid of honor takes the bride's bouquet or the best man hands the groom the bride's ring). Whether you're reading a poem or playing an instrument, there are specifics you'll need to cover at the rehearsal—for instance, "How will my poem get to the lectern? Do I have to carry it?" or "How do I lower the microphone for my oboe solo?"

Also, everyone in the wedding party has a designated position once he or she reaches the end of the aisle. Depending on the denomination of the ceremony, the bride and groom and all of their attendants each have preassigned positions in the ceremony. Making neat little formations isn't easy (have you ever noticed on television how drill sergeants make enlisted men do all that marching?) and it will definitely take practice to get it just right. The following are the most common formations:

### PROTESTANT

Officiant

Maid of honor        Best man

**Bride**    **Groom**

*Flower girl*     *Ring bearer*
*(optional)*      *(optional)*

| Bridesmaid | | | | | | Usher |
|---|---|---|---|---|---|---|
| | Bridesmaid | | | | Usher | |
| | | Bridesmaid | | Usher | | |
| | | Bridesmaid | Usher | | | |
| | | | Bridesmaid   Usher | | | |

An alternative to this formation is when the officiant has his or her back to the guests and the couple, the maid of honor, and the best man face out. The attendants then form a semicircle around them, also facing the guests.

### CATHOLIC

The positioning for the Catholic ceremony is identical to that of the Protestant ceremony.

## JEWISH

In a Jewish ceremony, the bride, the groom, their parents, and the honor attendants all stand under the *chupah*, or wedding canopy. The ushers and bridesmaids stand neatly around the fringes of the *chupah* (after all, there is only so much room under a little canopy), and the grandparents sit down in the first row and take a load off (*oy vay!*). The following is the standard formation around the *chupah*:

Rabbi/Cantor

| Groom's father | | | Bride's father |
|---|---|---|---|
| Groom's mother | | | Bride's mother |
| Best Man | **Groom** | **Bride** | Maid of honor |
| Usher | | | Bridesmaid |
| Usher | *Ring bearer* | *Flower girl* | Bridesmaid |
| Usher | *(optional)* | *(optional)* | Bridesmaid |
| Usher | | | Bridesmaid |
| Usher | | | Bridesmaid |

## The Recessional

You know the old saying: What goes up, must come down. Well, once everyone has marched down the aisle and the couple has said their "I do's," you have to go back up the aisle in order to leave the ceremony site and get to the bash that follows. Consult the following to figure out your place in each:

## PROTESTANT

**First—The happy couple.** The groom on the left, the bride on his right.

**Second—The ring bearer and the flower girl.** The flower girl should be on the ring bearer's right.

**Third—The maid of honor and the best man.** The maid of honor is on the best man's right side.

**Fourth—The first of the bridesmaids and the ushers.** The bridesmaid and usher closest to the center aisle are the first to leave. The bridesmaid will be on the usher's right. (If there

are more bridesmaids than ushers, the usher can escort two bridesmaids at once).
**Fifth—The rest of the bridesmaids and ushers.**

After the recessional, the maid of honor joins the bride, the groom, the best man, and the officiant in the signing of the marriage certificate, and then finally you're off to the reception. (Party, party, party!)

### CATHOLIC

Same as the Protestant recessional.

### JEWISH

In a Jewish recessional, the order is as follows, always with the female on the left:
**First—The happy couple.**
**Second—The bride's parents.**
**Third—The groom's parents.**
**Fourth—The ring bearer and the flower girl.**
**Fifth—The maid of honor and the best man.**
**Sixth—The bridesmaids and ushers.** The bridesmaid and usher closest to the center aisle are the first to leave. The others pair up and filter out behind them in kind.
**Seventh—The rabbi and the cantor.** The cantor is on the rabbi's left.

As you can see, everybody has his or her place in a wedding; rehearsing the ceremony gives the entire party a chance to familiarize themselves with the flow of the ceremony and to get comfortable with their parts. Remember, a confident bridesmaid is a happy (and smiling) bridesmaid.

## THE REHEARSAL DINNER

The rehearsal dinner follows the rehearsal. The groom's parents usually throw this event, but it can be given by someone from the bride's side or even just a close friend. The dinner can be attended by just the bridal party, or it can be open to all the out-of-town guests who have come for the wedding the following day. In a Christian ceremony, the groom's parents are not a part of the processional or recessional and as such, it is not necessary for them to participate in the wedding rehearsal itself; however, they are always included in the rehearsal dinner.

If no bridesmaid luncheon has been given, either by the bride or the bridesmaids, it is at the rehearsal dinner that the bride gives her attendants a gift, thanking them for throwing the bridal shower, for assisting her in putting together the wedding, and for accepting an active role in the occasion.

Most important, the rehearsal dinner not only represents a meal for those tired souls who are exhausted from rehearsing for the big event; it is also an opportunity for the bridal party and close family to toast the bride and groom in a more intimate setting.

The rehearsal dinner is a great opportunity to share personal memories of the bride and/or the groom (not too personal, of course; remember that the bride's parents are listening and they may not appreciate the story about how Laura accidentally left her diaphragm out on the kitchen counter that time you had the Tupperware party) and to make any presentations you may have planned. One bridesmaid we know prepared a slide show of pictures of both the bride and groom growing up. Another bridesmaid presented the bride with a handmade ivory silk bag for the bride to carry on her wedding day. The rehearsal dinner is a much more informal setting than the wedding and is a wonderful occasion for sharing memories of the bride and groom with a more intimate group of friends and family.

# CHAPTER NINE
# At the Wedding

VETERANS OF WWII recount experiencing a "battlefield high" on D-Day, an intensity of purpose combined with a camaraderie never duplicated again.

## THE WEDDING DAY

The shower was glorious, the bachelorette party was a bash, the rehearsal went off without a hitch, and you received a beautiful Elsa Perpetti pendant as a gift from the bride for your services. With the help of Valium or meditation and herbal tea, you've gotten a good night's rest. Your nails haven't chipped yet and that blemish on your chin is finally disappearing. Even the raspberry-colored taffeta bridesmaid gown looks kind of fetching in the light of the new day. You're feeling in control and confident. You've been training for months, preparing and planning. Yessiree, W-Day is looking pretty manageable from the toasty confines of your bed.

Well, pardon the wake-up call, but the real battle still lies ahead. You've survived basic training but, as a bridesmaid, the wedding is where you pull together everything you've learned in boot camp. All of your preparation, your meticulous planning—today is the day you will use it.

If you've planned well and prepared thoughtfully, you should be able to make it through this day with very few problems (barring acts of God and those little things that lawmaker named Murphy always talks about). If not, well, there's still time to make up for it. Consult the maid of honor as early in the day as possible (wake her up at the crack of dawn if you have to) and get the plan for the day. You're a modern woman—have her fax it to you. Then follow the checklist below, gather your things together, and get your butt out the door.

---

SUPERSTITIONS:   If the bride writes the names of her unmarried friends on the sole of her shoe before she walks down the aisle, the name that rubs off first will be the next person to get married.

---

## WEDDING-DAY CHECKLIST

- **Wedding Survival Kit** (see Chapter Two)
- Dress
- Shoes
- Two pairs of pantyhose or stockings/garter belt
- Directions (with any emergency contact phone numbers)
- Invitation
- Makeup
- Handbag
- Underwear (optional)
- Bra/bustier
- Required headgear/extra ponytail holder or barrette
- Extra change (for phone calls) and a few twenty-dollar bills (like your mother always told you—"just in case!")
- Camera/film

## PRIMPING

Primping with the bride and the other bridesmaids is one of the best parts of being in the wedding party. You're sitting around with the girls, chatting and munching on snacks, while people play with your hair. There is a lot of excitement surrounding a wedding. When a friend's marriage is about to become a reality and you are a member of the wedding party, you're in the thick of it all. Break out the camera and take pictures.

If you are getting your hair done professionally, wear a button-down shirt. One dedicated bridesmaid we know spent a small fortune to have her hair done at a salon alongside the bride. Her hair looked gorgeous, but how in the world was she supposed to take off her tiny T-shirt without mussing the new coif? Another bridesmaid had to cut the shirt off her body!

---

CELEBRITY TRIVIA:   When she wed Senator John F. Kennedy in 1953, Jacqueline Bouvier's bridesmaids wore pink silk faille and red satin gowns created by African-American designer Ann Lowe. Jackie's sister Lee Radziwill served as her matron of honor a second time when she wed Aristotle Onassis in 1968.

---

## "CHEESE!"

Formal wedding photographs are the bane of every bridesmaid's existence. You're on your feet wearing spiked heels in soft grass, standing totally stiff in a dress that's too tight, attempting to hold a smile while the photographer asks you to "turn this way" for about the 400th time. You're trying to banish thoughts of pulling an Alec Baldwin and putting your fist through his camera lens when the photographer finally says, "Okay, now the ushers." Ah, sweet relief.

Professional photos are a prerequisite of almost every wedding. Whether the pictures are taken by Bachrach or the groom's second cousin, formal photos capture everyone looking their best and provide the bride and groom, as well as the rest of the wedding party, with a special and irreplaceable memento of the wedding day.

While the bride will most likely have given the photographer a list of photos she particularly wants taken, many of which will include the bridal party, be sure to ask the bride for a photograph with her alone and make sure she gets one with all of her female attendants. Chances are that in the flurry of the millions of things the bride has tried to prepare for, she may have forgotten to request these two shots and she'll be grateful that you reminded her. These two photos make great keepsakes for you and the bride. Whatever you do, don't go directly to the photographer and start requesting pictures of you with your boyfriend. He or she is hired by the bride and groom, under their instruction, and is there to capture their day, not your good side. If you start insisting on certain photos, you might detract from what the bride and groom really want. If there is a photo you would really like taken, there is plenty of time at the reception to place yourself in front of the photographer's lens.

---

CELEBRITY TRIVIA:   Carolyn Bessette chose John F. Kennedy, Jr.'s sister, Caroline Schlossberg, and not one of her own, to serve as her matron of honor at their secluded 1996 wedding.

---

## TRIPPING DOWN THE AISLE: THE PROCESSIONAL

Well, you've practiced your march and you know your position. All that's left to do is focus on the end of the aisle, smile, and try not to trip. The following are a few helpful hints for marching gracefully down the aisle:

- For a Christian processional, leave three or four pews between you and the pair in front of you.
- For a Jewish processional, leave half the length of the aisle (unless instructed otherwise).
- Don't hum to the music.
- Be careful of runners, as they tend to scrunch up.
- Don't blatantly scan the congregation for your friends.
- Don't drag your feet.
- Don't drag your partner.
- Don't make small talk with your partner, even if he *is* cute. There's plenty of time for that at the reception.

# HE DOES, SHE DOES: THE CEREMONY

OK, you've successfully maneuvered your way down the aisle, you've all formed an almost perfect V shape, and a roomful of strangers are now staring back at you. You feel very important. The following hints are designed to help you maintain that facade of poise:

- Don't chat with your neighbor—even if she is dying to tell you about how she left the rehearsal dinner with the best man.
- Don't swing your flowers.
- If you have to blow your nose, do so discreetly (hide a tissue in your hand under your bouquet before you go down the aisle). Dabbing is better than blowing.
- Don't clear your throat when the officiant asks if anyone objects to the union.
- Do try to look interested in the ceremony. Or inspired. Or just serene.

# WHAT GOES UP, MUST COME DOWN: THE RECESSIONAL

Finally . . . on to the reception! The best advice we can give here is don't turn a stately walk down the aisle into a mad dash in a fervor to get to that punch bowl. (See Chapter Eight.)

# THE RECEPTION

## The Receiving Line

As guests begin to filter in to the reception, most likely, if there are more than 50 guests, there will be a receiving line to greet them. The order goes like this:

First in line—Bride's mother
Second in line—Bride's father (optional)
Third in line—Groom's mother
Fourth in line—Groom's father (optional)
Fifth in line—Bride
Sixth in line—Groom
Seventh in line—Maid of honor
Eighth in line (and so on . . . )—Bridesmaids (they may stand in
  any order they choose)

---

SUPERSTITIONS:  An old wives' tale says that if your younger sister gets married first, you have to dance barefoot at her wedding or you'll never find a husband.

---

## The Party!

Once the guests have been properly greeted and have had their opportunity to hug the mothers and kiss the bride, FINALLY it's time to party. Everyone knows that the reception is the big party that follows the ceremony, where the guests get to celebrate the marriage with the newlyweds. You mingle with the guests, drink to your heart's content, and dance till your feet hurt. Most wedding receptions follow a format similar to this one:

1. The bride and groom are introduced to the crowd.
2. The new couple dance first.
3. The parents and bridal party join the couple on the dance floor.
4. Everyone joins the bridal party on the dance floor.
5. Everyone sits down for the first course or salad (if a buffet is served, people begin to eat).
6. People dance.
7. The main course is served (if it's a buffet, people continue to eat).
8. People dance more.
9. The bride dances with her father.
10. The groom dances with his mother.

11. More dancing and drinking.
12. The bride and groom cut the cake.
13. Dessert is served (if it's a buffet, the grazing continues).
14. More dancing and drinking.
15. The bride tosses her bouquet.
16. The groom tosses the bride's garter.
17. The best man tosses his cookies.
18. The man who catches the garter puts it on the leg of the woman who caught the bouquet.
19. The reception comes to a close and the newlyweds take off for Tahiti.

It's perfectly okay to drink incessantly, line dance, and flirt with the drummer, but don't forget you're still on duty here and have obligations to the bride. Periodically check in with her and see if she needs you for anything. Make sure she gets something to eat (with all of that running around from table to table, her food may be whisked away by the waiters before she even tastes it); confirm that her makeup is holding up; help her into the bathroom if necessary. While you'll be satisfying the requirements of a bridesmaid, you'll also be fulfilling the most important duty of all, having a great time.

---

SUPERSTITIONS:   Guests around the world throw rice or grain at the newlyweds to symbolize fertility and growth in their new life together.

---

## Your Date

This brings us to a very important and sensitive matter. What if you're attached and would like your significant other to attend the wedding as your date?

Bear in mind that it is not necessarily your "right" as a bridesmaid to invite a guest. Guest lists are carefully compiled with a sharp eye on the bottom line; relationships are weighed against the cost per head quoted to the bride and groom by the caterers. If you are not invited with a guest, it isn't because the bride hates your boyfriend (at least that shouldn't be the reason). It's more likely that the reception hall can hold only so many people, and the guest list must be limited accordingly. Guest lists are like tiered wedding cakes; intimate family and closest friends are on top, and very extended family and acquaintances are on the bottom. Sounds simple, but think about how the bride's second cousin Trisha will feel if second cousin Lisa is invited and she isn't. The point is that people are invited in groups. If one person from the group is omitted, then they are doubly offended when they discover that people on the same tier are holding invitations to the big event. This applies to boyfriends and significant others as well. The bride and groom can't invite one person with a guest and then tell another guest that they cannot bring a date.

While you may be thinking, "But it's only one person," think again. There are probably ten other people who would like to bring dates; ten people is the equivalent of an additional table. For moderate-sized weddings of approximately 100–150 guests, the line today is typically drawn at engaged couples or live-in partners. Smaller weddings will preclude all guests except for spouses; larger weddings usually allow for guests to bring the milkman if they so please. If you feel strongly about having your significant other by your side at the wedding, it is acceptable to ask the bride if you may bring a date, but be conscientious and make it clear that you understand her dilemma.

If the bride agrees, you have another potential problem on your hands. You are, after all, on duty; being at someone else's beck and call doesn't always make for the greatest date. Often a date is brushed aside due to bridesmaid responsibilities—he can't sit with his date at dinner because she's at the table for the wedding party, he's in limbo during the formal pictures, and so on. For more established relationships, leaving your date to fend for himself isn't much of a problem. However, if your date is someone relatively new (we know of a bridesmaid who had a first date at a wedding) and hasn't met your friends, you may have bitten off more than you can chew. If you are considering bringing a date to the wedding, respond to the following statements with a "yes" or "no" to determine if you are better off going stag:

```
Y   N
—   —   1. I have met my date at least twice before.
—   —   2. My date knows my bra size.
—   —   3. My date has met the bride and/or the groom.
—   —   4. My date is friendly with the bride and/or the groom.
—   —   5. My date knows other people who will be at the wed-
           ding.
—   —   6. My date has seen me naked in the daylight.
—   —   7. My date calls me by a pet name.
—   —   8. My date calls parts of me by a pet name.
```

If you responded "yes" to more than five of these statements, you should know your significant other well enough to know whether or not he would have fun at the wedding even though your attention is drawn elsewhere. If you responded "no" to more than five, think twice before you bring that date. You'll be in the thick of the wedding festivities and he'll feel out of place; you may even feel burdened. If you answered "no" to *all* of the above, GO SOLO! You'll have a better chance of getting lucky with the bandleader.

For a single bridesmaid, a wedding is a great place to find a date. You're in the limelight; you're perfectly coiffed; people are asking you to dance. And we've never heard of anyone being rude to a bridesmaid (it's right up there with cursing at a nun). Use the opportunity to walk up to that cute guy at the bar and tell him it's a bridesmaid's duty to dance with every single man at the wedding. It's easier to be bold when you're wearing a brightly colored taffeta dress. Take advantage of your position and keep a pen and paper in your garter belt.

SUPERSTITIONS:   In some rural Chinese villages, sugar cane is tied together with ribbons representing wishes for the bride and groom's life together to be sweet.

## Catching the Bouquet

The throwing of the bridal bouquet is one of the most common reception traditions. There are several theories as to where the custom of the bouquet toss originated. One belief stems from early England, when it was believed that the bride was endowed with the power to transmit good luck to another person. People at the wedding tried to tear away bits of her clothing, and tried to snatch her flowers and headpiece. In self-defense she would throw her bouquet to the grabby crowd. In fourteenth-century France, throwing your bouquet was considered more demure than tossing your undergarments (garter). Either way, the belief was that the single woman who caught the bouquet would be the next to marry.

Unfortunately, for every winner, there are numerous losers; in order for one woman to walk away from the toss triumphant, the rest of the single women have to return to their seats, dejected. Due to the advances of feminism in recent years, many brides have chosen to forgo this tradition, which holds maidens up as poor pathetic creatures who need a man in their life. And grateful women around the country have heaved a collective sigh of relief.

However, many brides like to stick with tradition and feel compelled to include this ceremonial toss in their reception schedule. As a bridesmaid, it is important to note that if you are single, you must participate. You don't have to make an enthusiastic dive for the posies, but you should at least put your arms up at half mast. Of course, if you really just *can't* bear the ritual, hide out in the bathroom until it's over.

## Toasting the Bride and Groom

Though toasting the bride and groom is traditionally the bailiwick of the best man and the father of the bride, many people are so moved at a wedding that they feel compelled to speak. While the bride and groom have most likely worked out a schedule of toasts with the band, these impromptu speeches are a common occurrence as the evening wanes and the liquor disappears. If you are the honor attendant, you may want to express your best wishes for the couple ahead of time. Giving a toast can be a very nerve-wracking experience; even the most articulate people get awfully tongue-tied when they're full of emotion and champagne. As a bridesmaid, however, you are not obligated to give a toast at the wedding and should really only do so if no one else from the bride's side is planning to make a toast, and if the general consensus among the other bridesmaids is that you should be the spokesperson. If you do decide before the wedding that you will get up and speak at the reception, we recommend that you put together a few well-chosen words ahead of time. If you are inspired to speak in the heat of the moment, just try to keep it simple. Branching off into detailed recollections about your shared youth with the groom and playing doctor in his garage may make the guests squirm in their chairs. Resist the temptation to blabber, and try to keep your toast short. Food gets cold and people get bored. If you can't keep it short, put it in a letter and give it to the bride and groom after the wedding.

## Toasting Tips

- Shared childhood or school memories are always a touching source of material upon which to base a toast.
- Simple congratulations and well-wishing work nicely too.
- Speak up so everyone in back can hear you.

---

SUPERSTITIONS: Something old, something new, something borrowed, something blue: this superstition is perhaps the most recognized. The "old" represents the good luck of the bride's single life being carried into her married life; the "new" symbolizes her new life with her husband; "borrowed" is the tie that binds her to friends and community; and "blue" is for purity and fidelity.

---

# CHAPTER TEN

# When Things Go Awry

*A host is like a general; it takes a mishap to reveal his genius.*

—HORACE

UNFORESEEN EVENTS, in weddings as in war, can mar the best-laid plans. The ever-vigilant bridesmaid anticipates the unexpected and is always ready to spring to action. As a bridesmaid, you are a deputy hostess—a responsibility all the more urgent when the bride is suddenly indisposed or when things go awry. Brides have been known to faint when wedding tents collapse, rings are lost, or florists deliver the wrong flowers. This is your time to shine. The wedding disaster is an opportunity for the bridesmaid to show her mettle and prove she is more than just another pretty face. The old and young will gaze upon you in wonder and ask in awestruck tones, "Who is that bonneted maiden?" You will go down in family history as the spirited heroine who helped avert a crisis with her quick thinking and good humor. Or at least the bride will be really grateful. Of course, there are some instances when an extraordinary bridesmaid is the unsung heroine. With absolute discretion, she takes measures to ensure that no one ever finds out the nature of the calamity that she has forestalled.

You've heard the stories from friends and sisters who have returned from the field. Sometimes the bride has tantrums. She hurls her new china at the groom when he nonchalantly observes that his ex-wife registered for the same pattern. She isn't talking to her future in-laws because they want to serve whitefish at the rehearsal dinner. She's fired the priest because he won't refer to God as "She" during the service. Overnight, a fun-loving single woman has transformed into the finicky future Mrs. Fuss, lamenting aloud when surrounded by well-intentioned friends that nothing is as perfect as she had imagined it would be. Reaching for an ever-changing vision, she tears more pages out of *Bride* magazine and runs to the bridal shop to select new bridesmaid gowns hours before the wedding, or she dictates that all bridesmaids must report to the beauty salon for lime-green manicures. Never mind that they are wearing elbow-length gloves! Yes, sometimes the bride goes mad, and you'd better expect it. Roll your eyes when she's not watching and cluck sympathetically—but proceed, because it is your task to help turn the wheels of the great marriage machine.

Occasionally the bride's behavior is exemplary, and what goes wrong has nothing to do with her whatsoever. Of course, you could be the most capable, stalwart bridesmaid on earth, but a confluence of events—weather, roadblocks, bad hair—can conspire to make *you* look bad. Sometimes beyond etiquette, above manners, a bridesmaid needs ingenuity to help her cope. What to do when the mudpack hits the fan? Here are some stories about disasters major and minor that feature bridesmaids who either rescued the bride from years of psychoanalysis, or who, in retrospect, wish they'd been a little more alert. These heroic and cautionary tales will remind you to remain calm when confronted with any crisis on that red-letter day.

### Case #1: The Broken Engagement

Teddy Simpson and Alexandra Albright were the perfect romantic couple and for seven years had been the envy of many of their friends. Continuing a great family tradition, they met during their junior year at Princeton, where Mr. and Mrs. Simpson had met and where Mr. Albright had first laid eyes on Mrs. Albright. Their parents were such major benefactors that the college president happily gave their children personal parking lots. For two years, Teddy's hunter-green Triumph sat cozily next to Alexandra's orange Karmann Ghia as Teddy and Alexandra strolled hand in hand along the paths of the idyllic campus.

When they graduated, Teddy gave Alexandra his grandmother's emerald-and-diamond ring. Their mothers began planning the wedding. Teddy went to Harvard for his MBA and Alexandra took an assistant's job at Sotheby's. Shortly after Teddy became an associate at Morgan Stanley, 350 family friends received the long-awaited wedding invitations. Ten of Alexandra's girlfriends were fitted for bridesmaid dresses at the Vera Wang Salon on Madison Avenue. Then, four days before the wedding, all the invited guests received Federal Express packages with an announcement that read, "Mr. and Mrs. Chase Albright announce that the marriage of their daughter Alexandra Wells Albright to Mr. Theodore Burke Simpson, by mutual agreement, will not take place."

Only the maid of honor, Siobhan O'Reilly, knew the details of the drama that had gone on behind oak-paneled doors. Shortly after Alexandra had moved to New York, she met an Arab importer who whisked her away on a magic-carpet ride of the world's glittering cities every weekend she didn't dutifully board Amtrak to visit Teddy in Cambridge. Teddy no longer seemed to offer the same excitement and, more infuriatingly, had developed a habit of patting her on the head and giving her a peck on the cheek before dozing off every night. When Alexandra confided to Siobhan that it had been six months since she and Teddy had done anything more strenuous in bed than pass sections of the Sunday paper to each other, Siobhan sat her down and poured some brandy into her tea. It didn't take Alexandra long to realize that she didn't want to go to every Princeton homecoming game for the next 30 years with Teddy, though he had been her first love. She gave Teddy his ring back and named her first child Siobhan al Hussein, after the friend who made her open her eyes. Teddy is happily married to a woman he never makes love to with the lights on. The Simpson parents still do not talk to the Albrights.

*Moral*: Be an intuitive bridesmaid. All brides have last-minute jitters, but some have grave second thoughts that need to be aired. Listen sympathetically and tell the bride she'll have your support no matter what. If she wants to back out, there will be some hell to pay, but nothing so terrible as what she would go through in a divorce. A canceled wedding is an awkward and sad time, even if some of the major players are terribly relieved. Whether you hear firsthand, by letter, or by phone, don't ask a lot of impertinent questions that will compound somebody's humiliation and never, ever let on that you were there when it happened.

## Case #2: The Lost Groom

The morning of Josh and Laura's wedding, Josh disappeared. His parents were distressed, but hesitant to call Laura and give her what could only be upsetting news. They roused a stuporous Jamie, his brother and best man, who confessed he could not recall anything about the bachelor party the night before. Fortunately their sister, Amy, had overheard Jamie's plans for the night's activities. She retrieved an unconscious Josh from the floor of a downtown topless bar and dropped him off at home before driving to Laura's house to join the other bridesmaids. Amy never mentioned the pathetic but harmless incident to Laura and received a round-trip ticket to Aruba from her appreciative brother.

*Moral*: If the couple really loves each other, don't let them see each other in a negative light in the hectic days leading up to the event that will forever join their fates.

## Case #3: The Broken Arm

Bonnie was a very athletic, outdoorsy kind of girl. When she got engaged, her friends thought it would fun to throw her a ski shower, even though it was April and they all lived in San Francisco. Everyone brought a ski-related gift—long underwear instead of lingerie, new ski poles, certificates for lift tickets, and so on. One bridesmaid bought her roller blades. Bonnie eagerly bounded down the stairs and laced them up. Off she zoomed down the hill, blond hair flying. Twenty endless minutes ticked by on the hallway clock before the bridesmaids began exchanging glances. They found her two miles away, clutching her elbow and receiving affectionate licks from the basset hound that had gotten in her way. Her white cast matched her wedding dress, but she and the groom had to make alternate honeymoon plans, as their ski vacation in Peru was out of the question.

*Moral*: Don't let the bride use her shower gifts until after she is married.

## Case #4: The Couple on the Lam

Thomas's parents, blue-collar Long Island Catholics, were upset that his wedding to Ruth was not going to be held in their church. Her parents, Orthodox Jewish psychiatrists, had insisted on a synagogue miles away in New Jersey. Thomas and Ruth heard nothing but dire warnings from their parents about what a mismatched pair they were and endured months of grilling about how they would raise their as-yet-unborn children. Finally, in exasperation, Thomas and Ruth enlisted the help of their attendants to plan their elopement. Sans parents, Ruth and Thomas, along with the maid of honor and best man, flew to Las Vegas to be married. The attendants remaining in New Jersey made up excuses for the couple's absence until the deed was done.

*Moral*: Sometimes attendants may be called upon to perform *in absentia*. The most celebratory wedding doesn't have to be the wedding that happened the way it was planned.

## Case #5: The Bride and the Best Man

The music was already playing, but the bride, Linda, hadn't reappeared after exclaiming that she'd left her blue garter in her bedroom and running back to her parents' house. Nancy, the maid of honor, couldn't find Linda in her room, and slowly walked back downstairs. Pausing by the library doors, she heard Linda's voice. Relieved, she swung open the door, only to stop herself short from entering. Linda, in her wedding dress, was on the leather sofa, nibbling the best man's earlobe! Aghast, a blushing Linda tried to explain herself to Nancy as the best man adjusted himself with a rakish grin. Nancy held out a firm hand and shook her head. "Linda, don't give me any bullshit. You're stressed and you've momentarily lost your mind. Fix your lipstick and get your derrière outside." Linda ran past Nancy, who in one motion took a bold step forward and slapped the out-of-town best man across his too-handsome face. "This never happened and you're on the next flight out of here." She turned on her peach *peau de soie* heel and made it back to the processional line without a hair in her chignon out of place.

*Moral*: See the Moral for Case #2. Keep a level head and be prepared for all kinds of hijinks. Don't let the bride's behavior faze you.

## Case #6: The Pesky Parasite

Alicia's dream was to be married in a redwood forest. Her bridesmaids agreed that this would be an enchanted wedding—until the mosquitoes descended upon them as the couple exchanged vows. Knowing they were being videotaped, the young ladies valiantly smiled while suffering a thousand stings. Then they spied a mosquito the size of a small sparrow alight on Alicia's bare back. The maid of honor bravely stepped forward and swatted the offending insect, realizing that to preserve the bride's unblemished back was of higher priority than affecting a seamless, agonizing performance for a tape that could be edited.

*Moral*: Know your territory and be prepared. In this case, it would have been sensible for the bridal party to share a can of bug repellent before donning their wedding outfits. At a beach, sunscreen is essential. For a wedding in New York, bring Mace, in Los Angeles, an oxygen inhaler.

## Case #7: The Pregnant Maid of Honor

When Allison agreed to be Cynthia's maid of honor, she never anticipated that Cynthia's wedding would be postponed and rescheduled so that Cynthia could book her reception at the darling inn she and her fiancé had discovered only three weeks before their original wedding date. A year after the original date, Allison had married her longtime beau and was enceinte. In her fifth month, she was starting to show. At a second shower for the still-bride-to-be Cynthia, Allison mentioned that she was having her dress for Cynthia's wedding altered to accommodate her new shape. Cynthia cleared her throat and studied her reflection in the bread knife. "Allie," Cynthia began, "you'll be eight months pregnant on my big day . . . it wouldn't look right next to the other bridesmaids. I thought we might have Richard's sister stand in for you." Cynthia had never been more than cordial to Richard's seventeen-year-old sister, Trini, who incidentally was very photogenic and very thin.

What could Allison do? When Cynthia asked her to be her maid of honor, Allison was still a single, svelte woman, and Cynthia was certainly entitled to include her future sister-in-law in her wedding party. Allison let Cynthia's rude comment hang in the air and endured the rest of the shower. The next day she phoned Cynthia and told her that she was mailing her the dress along with the original bill so Trini could reimburse her. She wished Cynthia well and said that she hoped Cynthia would understand if she wasn't feeling up to being at the ceremony. The day of the wedding, Allison and her husband sent Cynthia and Richard a lovely letter of congratulations.

*Moral*: Know the friends you pledge your assistance to, and be sure they are worthy of your love and patience. Don't let a fretful bride lead you down a path of increasing financial burdens and inconveniences. Strive for graciousness even when the bride behaves in a selfish or just plain undignified manner.

## Case #8: Bad Hair

The prospect of sharing a hairstylist with nine other women didn't appeal to Tawny, so she begged her regular hairdresser, the talented Josef, to fit her in for a last-minute appointment. She needed undivided attention for her long, temperamental tresses. In her bridesmaid dress, Tawny sped to the salon, where Josef coiffed her mane to perfection. Slightly late, she raced her fire-engine-red BMW convertible to get to the outdoor ceremony on time. One glance in the rearview mirror confirmed that the salon's hair spray was no match for 75-mph winds. While trying to fold a scarf over her elaborate 'do, Tawny smeared red nail lacquer on her nose. Undeterred, tires squealing, she parked in front of the Audubon club and made it to the rose garden as the music began. Two minutes later, before a single photograph had been taken, a bluebird flew overhead and left a slimy calling card atop Tawny's head.

*Moral*: Don't leave all your grooming preparations until the last minute. Unless you want to risk life, limb, and bouffant, leave yourself plenty of time to get to the altar. The bridesmaids' hair and nails should be done by a professional on site, or at a salon with prearranged transportation waiting. If you think hair is more important than being available for the bride before the ceremony, you should be a hairdresser, not a bridesmaid.

## Case #9: The Felonious Limousine Driver

The bride's family had arranged for a fleet of limousines to transport guests from the church to the reception. Four bridesmaids in one limo were alarmed when their driver took a left turn instead of following the other cars. They were furious when he joked that he was going to sell them into white slavery. One bridesmaid peeled off her pantyhose and blindfolded him while another grabbed the wheel. A third bridesmaid was able to call the police with the cellular phone hidden in her bouquet. Unflustered, they arrived in time for the wedding photographs.

*Moral*: Don't let a nutcase or a hijacking stop you from getting the job done. Your outfit is replete with weapons. Use a stiletto heel to bring the enemy to his knees; garrote him with an underwire brassiere; pierce his eardrum with a bobby pin. (See "Wedding Survival Kit" in Chapter Two.)

## Case #10: The Waltz That Wasn't

At a country-club wedding in Maine, a flamenco band showed up to substitute for the orchestra the bride had hired. There were many older folks at the wedding, and the bride and groom had felt that everyone would enjoy some big-band music. The bride was in tears and refused to enter the ballroom until she heard shouts of merriment accompanying the exotic music. Her bridesmaids were teaching her uncles, all in their seventies, how to flamenco! She decided to follow in their footsteps and the dancing lasted until past midnight.

*Moral*: Always set an example for the less spontaneous with your flexibility and enthusiasm.

## Case #11: The Lecherous Photographer

After an hour of posing for wedding photographs, the bridesmaids realized that the photographer had positioned them so the afternoon sun was shining through their linen dresses, outlining their bare legs. Annoyed, one of the bridesmaids told him he'd have to reshoot the two rolls of film he had already taken. When he refused, she found a beefy usher who was only too happy to be of service. The photographer handed over the erotic film and performed his job as instructed for the rest of the session.

*Moral*: Take advantage of the one thing that ushers have to offer—brawn. Other than that, they primarily serve as decoration!

## Case #12: The Missing Crabs

A seafood-loving bride hired a caterer that was famous for his Cajun flavored soft-shell crabs. Her entire wedding carried out a Cajun theme. Unfortunately, the caterer's truck overheated en route to the reception. His assistant saved everything but the crabs. The New Orleans bride was devastated. Her maid of honor, a chef from New York, grabbed a local usher and ordered him to drive her to the area's largest fish store. She bought a mess of clams and rescued the reception with a Long Island–style clambake.

*Moral*: Share your hidden talents to save the day. Always find a safe man or woman to be your chauffeur in unfamiliar cities.

## Case #13: The Tidal Wave

At a wedding held on a Caribbean island during hurricane season, a ceremony was taking place aboard a yacht. Suddenly, a tidal wave broke over the side, leaving the entire wedding party drenched but unharmed. When the best man reached into his pocket for the wedding ring, he realized it had washed away. The next day, a plucky bridesmaid rented a metal detector and walked the entire perimeter of the island until she found the antique platinum ring.

*Moral*: You can never place enough importance on the ring.

Remember those folks who told you that no more is required of a bridesmaid than to look beautiful while walking up the aisle? These are the same clowns who, when giving directions to a local church in a countryside of rolling hills and winding roads, say to an out-of-towner in a rented car, "You can't miss it." You know better.

Every wedding represents an adventure from which dozens of anecdotes can be collected. The exemplary attendant stores away the most outrageous war stories for her granddaughter, imparting to her when she comes of age the wisdom of the guerrilla bridesmaid.

# CHAPTER ELEVEN
# The Party's Over

PSTD, Post-Traumatic Stress Disorder, is a reaction to a psychologically traumatic event outside the range of normal experience. It occurs erratically among veterans of war and manifests itself in recurrent nightmares, cold sweats when recollecting the battle experience, reluctance in deepening social relationships, feelings of guilt, and sleep disturbances.

The flower girl has caught the bouquet. The band is packing up. You've managed not to tear your dress while dancing and you've posed for candid shots with guests whose names you've forgotten. The bride and groom have thanked their parents and are on their way to a transatlantic honeymoon in a rented Bentley trailing shoes and soup cans. Rice is sticking to your hair. All is quiet in the jungle. Hey! The wedding is over.

You're feeling expansive, proud, and slightly deflated; you've survived and your performance merits an honorable discharge, but you feel you've lost a guerrilla to domesticity. You feel slightly older, but sense a new perspective developing within you about the value of family and the importance of hallowed traditions you once pooh-poohed. When ambivalence begins settling in and making you feel irritable, congratulate the parents, bid farewell to out-of-town relatives or far-flung friends, and get the hell out! Return to your hotel room or, preferably, directly home.

If you are single, avoid indulging in too much circumspection now, as it will lead to depression. Instead of mourning the loss of a single friend and the husband you think you'll never find, treat yourself to a hot bath and ponder your next hair-raising adventure. Remember that old German proverb: *Für jeden Topf, gibt es eine Dekel* ("For every lid, there is a pot"). Life is a banquet, and there are plenty of dishes you've yet to sample. So many men, so little time. If you are dating, relish the time you can spend with your beau that doesn't involve refereeing invitation-list-clutching mothers. Already married? Be grateful you've made it past that tough first year the couple is now entering and treat your husband to a night to remember.

As you mentally debrief yourself after the bridesmaid mission, follow these steps:

- Get rid of that dress! Rather than dumping it into the trash compactor, dry-clean it. A high-end cleaner will clean, spot-treat, and restore a gown to its original luster. Ask about an anti–sugar stain process that removes stubborn champagne and cake-icing stains. If the dress looks presentable, a consignment shop will give you half of whatever they receive for it. Also, thrift shops around the nation will take dresses in decent condition. You won't receive any money back but you can get a tax deductible and help a good cause at the same time. If you have a perverse sense of style, recycle the fabric for a pillow for your Labrador.
- Throw away the wilting flower arrangement you took from your table at the reception. Toss it sooner if it looks like Audrey II, the botanical specimen from *Little Shop of Horrors*.
- Make notes on how you would do a wedding differently.
- Sort through the phone numbers you collected from the ushers—but don't call the suave one who smelled of Aqua Velva.
- Regale friends who don't know the bride with wedding anecdotes.
- Look forward to getting together with the bride when she comes back from her honeymoon full of stories.
- Rent movies or watch TV sitcoms that celebrate or will make you cling to the single life: *Auntie Mame, First Wives Club, Fatal Attraction, All in the Family, Married . . . With Children*.

If you find yourself suffering from PWSD (Post-Wedding Stress Disorder), try therapy in one of these forms: strawberry Häagen-

Dazs, an Italian black lace teddy, a new hair color, a Swedish massage from a man named Sven, Manolo Blahnik heels.

You are now ready to resume your life as a civilian!

---

SUPERSTITIONS: If you sleep on a piece of the groom's cake, which in many cultures are handed out at the reception as favors, it is believed that your future spouse will come to you in your dreams.

---

# CHAPTER TWELVE
# Just Say No

A CONSCIENTIOUS objector refuses on moral or religious grounds to bear arms in a military conflict or to serve in the armed forces. An objector is willing to risk the scorn of peers and authority figures rather than compromise her value system. A draft dodger evades compulsory military service without officially stating her reasons, often by fleeing over a border.

Unfortunately, this is one of those things in life that is "just not done." If someone asks you to be her bridesmaid, assume she considers you to be one of her closest friends. If you are her sister, remember that the two of you are supposed to be close. Refusing is tantamount to saying, "I don't care to be a member of your intimate circle celebrating the most important day of your life." It's impolite. If you can say these words without concern for the consequent damage, refuse without a second thought. However, if you want to preserve the relationship without offering this level of commitment, read on.

We realize that whether it's due to your fabulous networking or because you've been holding onto the remnants of a friendship you've outgrown, it can happen that a woman has cheerfully put you on her "A" list of friends, whereas if you could just remember her last name, you might find room only on your "C" list. Sigh. The price one pays for possessing charisma. If you can't nobly accept the honor of serving as this well-intentioned bride's attendant because you know you will stumble most ignominiously in fulfilling your duties, it is far more gracious to find a credible excuse right away to avoid the whole affair. Better to risk a "tsk-tsk" now than to provoke a chorus of hisses later.

Perhaps there are extenuating circumstances—a scheduling conflict, lack of funds, or a death in the family—that prevent you from serving. A true friend will appreciate your honesty if you say, "I am so honored, but I just can't *afford* to participate the way I would like to as a bridesmaid. Would you settle for me as a guest?" Or whatever your heartfelt cop-out is. Practice in front of a mirror or with a tape recorder until you look and sound firm and unable to be swayed. Practice, practice, practice.

With apologies to Miss Manners, we offer these unreproachable excuses:

> "I am scheduled for a Cesarean that day and am expecting twins."
>
> "I testified against a Colombian drug cartel and am entering a witness protection program."
>
> "I was once engaged to your fiancé and he left me when I developed a yeast infection."
>
> "That's the week of my honeymoon! I'll be in Rialto."

Do you get the idea? Seize upon a life-and-death scenario, non-refundable plane tickets, or a critical business trip. Good luck. And watch out for dogs at the border.

# THE BRIDESMAID'S DIARY:
# A JOURNAL OF YOUR TOURS OF DUTY
## First Tour of Duty

Bride's/Groom's Names: _____

    Your Relation to Bride or Groom: _____

**Your Status:** *Bridesmaid/Maid of Honor/Mother of the Bride (circle one)*

Bridesmaid/Usher Count: _____

Bridesmaids' Names: _____

_____

Bridesmaid's Dress: _____

    Style/color/size: _____

    Purchased/disposed of at: _____

Engagement Gift: _____

Bridal Shower Details: _____

    Themes/games: _____

    Menu: _____

Bridal Shower Gift: _____

Bridal Shower Pitfalls/Successes: _____

_____

_____

Bridesmaids' Luncheon: _____

_____

Bachelorette Party: _____

_____

Rehearsal Dinner: _____

_____

Bridesmaid's Gift from Bride: _____

Wedding Details: _____

_____

Wedding Gift: _____

Additional Comments: _____

_____

## Second Tour of Duty

Bride's/Groom's Names: _____

   Your Relation to Bride or Groom: _____

**Your Status:** *Bridesmaid/Maid of Honor/Mother of the Bride (circle one)*

Bridesmaid/Usher Count: _____

Bridesmaids' Names: _____

_____

Bridesmaid's Dress: _____

   Style/color/size: _____

   Purchased/disposed of at: _____

Engagement Gift: _____

Bridal Shower Details: _____

   Themes/games: _____

   Menu: _____

Bridal Shower Gift: _____

Bridal Shower Pitfalls/Successes: _____

_____

_____

_____

Bridesmaids' Luncheon: _____

_____

Bachelorette Party: _____

_____

Rehearsal Dinner: _____

_____

Bridesmaid's Gift from Bride: _____

Wedding Details: _____

_____

_____

Wedding Gift: _____

Additional Comments: _____

_____

_____

## Third Tour of Duty

Bride's/Groom's Names: _____

   Your Relation to Bride or Groom: _____

**Your Status:** *Bridesmaid/Maid of Honor/Mother of the Bride (circle one)*

Bridesmaid/Usher Count: _____

Bridesmaids' Names: _____

_____

Bridesmaid's Dress: _____

   Style/color/size: _____

   Purchased/disposed of at: _____

Engagement Gift: _____

Bridal Shower Details: _____

   Themes/games: _____

   Menu: _____

Bridal Shower Gift: _____

Bridal Shower Pitfalls/Successes: _____

_____

_____

_____

Bridesmaids' Luncheon: _____

_____

Bachelorette Party: _____

_____

Rehearsal Dinner: _____

_____

Bridesmaid's Gift from Bride: _____

Wedding Details: _____

_____

_____

Wedding Gift: _____

Additional Comments: _____

_____

_____

## Fourth Tour of Duty

Bride's/Groom's Names: _____

   Your Relation to Bride or Groom: _____

**Your Status:** *Bridesmaid/Maid of Honor/Mother of the Bride (circle one)*

Bridesmaid/Usher Count: _____

Bridesmaids' Names: _____

_____

Bridesmaid's Dress: _____

   Style/color/size: _____

   Purchased/disposed of at: _____

Engagement Gift: _____

Bridal Shower Details: _____

   Themes/games: _____

   Menu: _____

Bridal Shower Gift: _____

Bridal Shower Pitfalls/Successes: _____

_____

_____

_____

Bridesmaids' Luncheon: _____

_____

Bachelorette Party: _____

_____

Rehearsal Dinner: _____

_____

Bridesmaid's Gift from Bride: _____

Wedding Details: _____

_____

_____

Wedding Gift: _____

Additional Comments: _____

_____

_____

## Fifth Tour of Duty

Bride's/Groom's Names: _____

   Your Relation to Bride or Groom: _____

**Your Status:** *Bridesmaid/Maid of Honor/Mother of the Bride (circle one)*

Bridesmaid/Usher Count: _____

Bridesmaids' Names: _____

_____

Bridesmaid's Dress: _____

   Style/color/size: _____

   Purchased/disposed of at: _____

Engagement Gift: _____

Bridal Shower Details: _____

   Themes/games: _____

   Menu: _____

Bridal Shower Gift: _____

Bridal Shower Pitfalls/Successes: _____

_____

_____

_____

Bridesmaids' Luncheon: _____

_____

Bachelorette Party: _____

_____

Rehearsal Dinner: _____

_____

Bridesmaid's Gift from Bride: _____

Wedding Details: _____

_____

_____

Wedding Gift: _____

Additional Comments: _____

_____

_____

## Sixth Tour of Duty

Bride's/Groom's Names: _____

    Your Relation to Bride or Groom: _____

**Your Status:** *Bridesmaid/Maid of Honor/Mother of the Bride (circle one)*

Bridesmaid/Usher Count: _____

Bridesmaids' Names: _____

_____

Bridesmaid's Dress: _____

    Style/color/size: _____

    Purchased/disposed of at: _____

Engagement Gift: _____

Bridal Shower Details: _____

    Themes/games: _____

    Menu: _____

Bridal Shower Gift: _____

Bridal Shower Pitfalls/Successes: _____

_____

_____

_____

Bridesmaids' Luncheon: _____

_____

Bachelorette Party: _____

_____

Rehearsal Dinner: _____

_____

Bridesmaid's Gift from Bride: _____

Wedding Details: _____

_____

_____

Wedding Gift: _____

Additional Comments: _____

_____

_____

## Seventh (whew!) Tour of Duty

Bride's / Groom's Names: _____

   Your Relation to Bride or Groom: _____

**Your Status:** *Bridesmaid / Maid of Honor / Mother of the Bride (circle one)*

Bridesmaid / Usher Count: _____

Bridesmaids' Names: _____

_____

Bridesmaid's Dress: _____

   Style / color / size: _____

   Purchased / disposed of at: _____

Engagement Gift: _____

Bridal Shower Details: _____

   Themes / games: _____

   Menu: _____

Bridal Shower Gift: _____

Bridal Shower Pitfalls / Successes: _____

_____

_____

_____

Bridesmaids' Luncheon: _____

_____

Bachelorette Party: _____

_____

Rehearsal Dinner: _____

_____

Bridesmaid's Gift from Bride: _____

Wedding Details: _____

_____

_____

Wedding Gift: _____

Additional Comments: _____

_____

_____

## Eighth Tour of Duty

Bride's/Groom's Names: _____

    Your Relation to Bride or Groom: _____

**Your Status:** *Bridesmaid/Maid of Honor/Mother of the Bride (circle one)*

Bridesmaid/Usher Count: _____

Bridesmaids' Names: _____

_____

Bridesmaid's Dress: _____

    Style/color/size: _____

    Purchased/disposed of at: _____

Engagement Gift: _____

Bridal Shower Details: _____

    Themes/games: _____

    Menu: _____

Bridal Shower Gift: _____

Bridal Shower Pitfalls/Successes: _____

_____

_____

_____

Bridesmaids' Luncheon: _____

_____

Bachelorette Party: _____

_____

Rehearsal Dinner: _____

_____

Bridesmaid's Gift from Bride: _____

Wedding Details: _____

_____

_____

Wedding Gift: _____

Additional Comments: _____

_____

_____

**Seventh (whew!) Tour of Duty**

Bride's/Groom's Names: _____

   Your Relation to Bride or Groom: _____

**Your Status:** *Bridesmaid/Maid of Honor/Mother of the Bride (circle one)*

Bridesmaid/Usher Count: _____

Bridesmaids' Names: _____

_____

Bridesmaid's Dress: _____

   Style/color/size: _____

   Purchased/disposed of at: _____

Engagement Gift: _____

Bridal Shower Details: _____

   Themes/games: _____

   Menu: _____

Bridal Shower Gift: _____

Bridal Shower Pitfalls/Successes: _____

_____

_____

_____

Bridesmaids' Luncheon: _____

_____

Bachelorette Party: _____

_____

Rehearsal Dinner: _____

_____

Bridesmaid's Gift from Bride: _____

Wedding Details: _____

_____

_____

Wedding Gift: _____

Additional Comments: _____

_____

_____

## Eighth Tour of Duty

Bride's/Groom's Names: _____

 Your Relation to Bride or Groom: _____

**Your Status:** *Bridesmaid/Maid of Honor/Mother of the Bride (circle one)*

Bridesmaid/Usher Count: _____

Bridesmaids' Names: _____

_____

Bridesmaid's Dress: _____

 Style/color/size: _____

 Purchased/disposed of at: _____

Engagement Gift: _____

Bridal Shower Details: _____

 Themes/games: _____

 Menu: _____

Bridal Shower Gift: _____

Bridal Shower Pitfalls/Successes: _____

_____

_____

_____

Bridesmaids' Luncheon: _____

_____

Bachelorette Party: _____

_____

Rehearsal Dinner: _____

_____

Bridesmaid's Gift from Bride: _____

Wedding Details: _____

_____

_____

Wedding Gift: _____

Additional Comments: _____

_____

_____

## Ninth Tour of Duty

Bride's/Groom's Names: _____

  Your Relation to Bride or Groom: _____

**Your Status:** *Bridesmaid/Maid of Honor/Mother of the Bride (circle one)*

Bridesmaid/Usher Count: _____

Bridesmaids' Names: _____

_____

Bridesmaid's Dress: _____

  Style/color/size: _____

  Purchased/disposed of at: _____

Engagement Gift: _____

Bridal Shower Details: _____

  Themes/games: _____

  Menu: _____

Bridal Shower Gift: _____

Bridal Shower Pitfalls/Successes: _____

_____

_____

_____

Bridesmaids' Luncheon: _____

_____

Bachelorette Party: _____

_____

Rehearsal Dinner: _____

_____

Bridesmaid's Gift from Bride: _____

Wedding Details: _____

_____

_____

Wedding Gift: _____

Additional Comments: _____

_____

_____

## Tenth Tour of Duty*

Bride's/Groom's Names: _____

   Your Relation to Bride or Groom: _____

**Your Status:** *Bridesmaid/Maid of Honor/Mother of the Bride (circle one)*

Bridesmaid/Usher Count: _____

Bridesmaids' Names: _____

_____

Bridesmaid's Dress: _____

   Style/color/size: _____

   Purchased/disposed of at: _____

Engagement Gift: _____

Bridal Shower Details: _____

   Themes/games: _____

   Menu: _____

Bridal Shower Gift: _____

Bridal Shower Pitfalls/Successes: _____

_____

_____

Bridesmaids' Luncheon: _____

_____

Bachelorette Party: _____

_____

Rehearsal Dinner: _____

_____

Bridesmaid's Gift from Bride: _____

Wedding Details: _____

_____

_____

Wedding Gift: _____

Additional Comments: _____

_____

* If you've made it this far, your copy of *The Bridesmaid's Guerrilla Handbook* must be extremely dog-eared. Time for a new copy!

# BIBLIOGRAPHY

Baldrige, Letitia. *Letitia Baldrige's Complete Guide to the New Manners for the '90s.* New York: Rawson Associates, 1990.

The Editors of *Bride's* magazine. *The Bridesmaid's Little Book of Customs & Keepsakes.* Clarkson Potter, 1994.

Claiborne, Craig. *Elements of Etiquette: A Guide to Table Manners in an Imperfect World.* New York: William Morrow and Co., 1992.

Clark, Beverly. *Showers: The Complete Guide to Hosting a Perfect Bridal Shower or Baby Shower.* Emeryville: Wilshire Publications, 1989.

Fussell, Paul. *Doing Battle: The Making of a Skeptic.* New York: Little Brown & Co., 1996.

Lee, Vera. *Something Old, Something New: What You Didn't Know about Wedding Ceremonies, Celebrations and Customs.* Illinois: Sourcebooks, 1994.

Lluch, Elizabeth, and Alex Lluch. *Wedding Party Responsibility Cards.* San Diego: Wedding Solutions, 1994.

Martin, Judith. *Miss Manners on Painfully Proper Weddings.* New York: Crown, 1995.

Naylor, Sharon. *1001 Ways to Save Money and Still Have a Dazzling Wedding.* Contemporary Books. 1994.

Packham, Jo. *Wedding Parties & Showers: Planning Memorable Celebrations.* New York: Sterling Publishing Co., 1993.

Post, Elizabeth L. *Emily Post on Weddings.* New York: Harper Collins, 1994.

# THE AUTHORS

**Sarah Stein**
Sarah graduated with honors from the University of Massachusetts at Amherst in 1988 and has worked in publishing for eight years. She has served as a bridesmaid seven times—once unjustly ousted (she swears she never touched him!), and three times as maid of honor. An amateur bridal consultant and aspiring bride-to-be turned newlywed, Sarah has successfully helped guide many happy brides down the aisle. She lives in New York City.

**Lucy Talbot**
Lucy graduated *magna cum laude* from Barnard College in 1990 and has worked in publishing for six years. She has served as a bridesmaid twice and a maid of honor once, with disastrous results. Lucy lives in New York City and plans to elope when the inevitable happens.